Nordic Modern Church & Chapel
Light in the Sacred Space

Photograph & Text Takashi KOIZUMI

北欧モダンチャーチ＆チャペル
聖なる光と祈りの空間

写真・文 小泉 隆

冬の凍てつくような寒さの中、遠くから教会に辿り着いた人達にとって
そこで眼にする暖かさや優しい雰囲気は
特別な価値を持つことでしょう

アルヴァ・アールト , 1920

"Warm and soft atmosphere may have special value in
the eyes of church goers especially when its freezing cold in the winter
and people come to church from long distances."

Alvar Aalto, 1920

教会において
光は単に賛美歌集を読むためのものではありません

ペーターセルシング

"Light in a church can not be only a light
to read lymn book by."

Peter Celsing

CONTENTS

Introduction	006	北欧モダンチャーチ＆チャペル 聖なる光と祈りの空間
Denmark	011	デンマーク
Sweden	049	スウェーデン
Finland	091	フィンランド
Norway	133	ノルウェー
Iceland	163	アイスランド
Appendix	175	解説・資料編
Topography and Climate of Nordic Countries	176	北欧諸国の地勢と気候
Four Seasons and the Light in Nordic Countries	178	北欧諸国の四季と光
Examples and map	182	事例リストと地図
References	185	参考図書文献
Postscript	186	あとがき

北欧モダンチャーチ＆チャペル
聖なる光と祈りの空間

小泉　隆

序

　夏の沈まない太陽、暗く長い冬の夜、太陽高度の低い光、オーロラの出現など、北極圏およびそこにほど近い北欧諸国[注1]には、北の地ゆえの特異な光環境が要因となって、独特の光の文化が醸成されている。

　建築物においても自然光の扱いに優れた建築、自然光の美しい空間が数多く存在する。とりわけ光が重要な要素となる教会に足を踏み入れると、この上なく美しい光と空間に魅了されることが多い。そこでは、北欧独特の光が巧みに懐柔されて、聖なる祈りの空間が作られている。

　本書は、著者が訪れたデンマーク、スウェーデン、フィンランド、ノルウェー、アイスランドにおける20世紀以降に建てられた教会および礼拝堂[注2]の中で、光と空間の豊かな例を、美しい瞬間を捉えた写真とともに紹介するものである。

　北欧諸国には、歴史ある教会建築[注3]も数多く存在する一方、近代から現代にかけても多くの教会や礼拝堂が建てられている。北欧諸国はキリスト教のルター派[注4]が主流であり、それらの建築表現はとても自由な印象を与える。ルーテル教会の権威や伝統にこだわらない姿勢や風潮、機能本位なところ、地域のコミュニティの場としての機能を持つことなどが、自由表現を生み出す、また受容する土壌になっているように思われる。

　もちろん北欧に限らずとも、またルーテル教会以外でもそのような建築は見受けられるが、カトリックを国教とする国々などと比べると、そのような表現の教会建築が数多く存在する地域と言えるであろう。

　また北欧諸国の20世紀以降に建てられた教会には、しっとりとその土地の風土に馴染み、歴史との連続性を保ちながら、信者達やそこを訪れる人々に愛情を持って使われ、日常において豊かさや美そして悦びをもたらしていることを実感できる良質な建築が数多く存在する。教会という特殊なビルディングタイプではあるが、次から次へと新しい建築が出来ては消費される現代において、「建築の在り方」を考える上で参考になる点が多いとも考える。

　北欧の各地に点在するそれらの教会の多くは、人間味や優しさ、落ち着きなど、北欧の建築全般に共通する雰囲気や特性を持ちながらも、それぞれの国や地域において、異なる気候風土、景観、生活文化、自然観などの影響、そして教会の在り方や建築家の個性などがその表現の違いに表れている。

　牧歌的な風景に佇む姿、険しい環境に対峙する姿勢、死と生に向き合う精神性、暗さの中に見いだされる神秘性、白い光に満ちた空間、森や水といった自然と共生する姿勢、礼拝の場とは思えない自由な感覚など。今回の事例からそのような共通性と多様性を楽しんでもらえればと思う。

　北の地の教会を訪れ、静けさの中、美しい光の空間に身を預け、その時々の光や外の自然を感じながら過ごしていると、ものに溢れ、忙しい現代に生きる我々にとっては、救われるような幸福な時間に包まれる。その体験が我々の生活を見直すなんらかのきっかけになるように思えてならない。

　本書がきっかけとなって、読者の皆様が北欧の教会の美しい光と空間を体験し、色々と思いを巡らして頂ければ、著者としては嬉しい限りである。

注 1)「北欧」あるいは「北欧諸国」(Nordic countries) とは、デンマーク、スウェーデン、フィンランド、ノルウェーの四カ国に、バルト三国、ブリテン諸島、そしてアイスランドを加えた国々をいう。しかしながら、一般にはデンマーク、スウェーデン、フィンランド、ノルウェーの四カ国あるいはそれにアイスランドを加えた五カ国を範囲として用いられている事が多い。本書ではその5カ国を対象としている。一方、スカンジナビア・デザインなどと言われるように、北欧諸国について「スカンジナビア (Scandinavia)」と呼ぶこともあるが、その場合は、スカンジナビア半島にあるデンマーク、スウェーデン、ノルウェーの3カ国が対象である。しかし「北欧」「北欧諸国」と混用され、その他の国々もその範囲に加えられて使用されている事も多い。

2)「教会」は、共通の信仰によって形成される集団や団体自体の意味と、その宗教活動の拠点となる施設・建物を意味するが、ここでは後者の意味とする。本書では一般的に「教会」と区別して呼ばれる、墓地や火葬場などに建てられている礼拝の単独施設である「礼拝堂」、修道士たちが共同生活する「修道院」も対象とした。教会、礼拝堂、修道院からなる建築群の総称としては「教会」を用い、各々の建築は、それらを区別して具体的な呼称で記す。本書では建物全体の中で「主たる礼拝のための空間」を中心的に扱う。その呼称は、建物種別や宗派などによって異なり、さらには英語表記との違いもある。
日本語表記は、プロテスタントにおいては教会建物内の「主たる礼拝のための空間」を「礼拝堂」と呼ぶことが一般的である。対して、カトリックや正教会では、主祭壇を囲む「主たる礼拝のための空間」を「礼拝堂」とは呼ばずに「聖堂」と呼ぶことが多い。聖堂とは別に内部や外部に存在する「副次的な礼拝の空間」を「礼拝堂」あるいは「礼拝室」と呼ぶ。修道院では「主たる礼拝のための空間」を「聖堂」「教会堂」と呼ぶことが多い。このように「主たる礼拝のための空間」を示す用語は、建物種別や宗派等により異なり複雑であるが、本書では基本的に「主たる礼拝のための空間」を「礼拝堂」と呼ぶことにした。
英語表記では、「chapel」は、カトリックや正教会などの副次的な礼拝空間や単独の礼拝施設に使われ、「主たる礼拝のための空間」を指す「礼拝堂」については、「church」「hall」などと表記することが多い。本書では、「主たる礼拝のための空間」に対して、日本語表記で「礼拝堂」と呼ぶものも、英語表記では、各事例の既往書などでの使用語を参照し、「建物全体」の呼称との関係にも注意し、適宜「church」「church interior」「church space」「hall」などと表記する。なお、副次的な礼拝の空間を指す「礼拝堂」あるいは「礼拝室」と、礼拝のための単独の施設「礼拝堂」の英語表記については「chapel」と記す。より厳密で詳細な内容については専門書を参照されたい。

3) 北欧諸国の古い教会建築に関しては、伊藤大介氏による次の説明がその全体像を理解するのに良いと考える。
「教会は北欧にとって、明らかに外来文化として始まり、まずはヨーロッパの様式が北欧の主要都市にもたらされた。そして次の段階として人々の信仰心を支えるものとなって地方の小さな村々にまで根づいていくのである。大聖堂の建設のために導入された様式は、導入のルートによって、"ドイツ風"も"フランス風"も("ロシア風"さえ) ありえたのが北欧であった。各国の様式が並立しているのは北欧ゆえの興味深い現象といえようが、これらは本当に定着したとは言いがたい面もあったかもしれない。その一方で村々に浸透して土着化した小さな教会は、"北欧風"などとひとくくりにできるものではなく、北欧各地のそれぞれの風土条件の中で固有の姿で根づいている。」そして、ノルウェーの木造スターブ教会、デンマークの白い階段状破風を持つ煉瓦造・石造の教会、フィンランド・スウェーデンの花崗岩の中世教会、フィンランドの近世木造教会などを後者の例としてあげている。
伊藤大介『図説北欧の建築遺産 都市と自然に育まれた文化』(河出書房新社、2010)

4) 北欧諸国では現在、信仰の自由が認められているが、キリスト教のルター派の信者が多勢を占めている。スウェーデンは2000年まで、ノルウェーは2012年まで福音ルーテル派教会が国教であった。そしてアイスランド、デンマークは、現在も福音ルーテル派教会が国教であり、フィンランドは福音ルーテル派教会とフィンランド正教会が国教である (2017年現在)。

Nordic Modern Church & Chapel
Light in the Sacred Space

Takashi KOIZUMI

Introduction

The midnight sun in summer, dark and long nights in winter, sunlight from a low solar elevation, and the appearance of the Aurora Borealis: due to the distinctive light environment of the northland, a unique culture of light has been fostered in the Arctic Circle and nearby Nordic countries[1].

As for architecture, there are many buildings superior in handling natural light, and many spaces with glorious natural light. In particular, when stepping into a church or a chapel, where light plays an important role, people are often fascinated by the most beautiful light and space. The unique Nordic light is dexterously tamed there, creating a holy space for praying.

With photos capturing moments of beauty, this book introduces examples of rich light and spaces in church buildings and chapels[2] built after the 20th century in countries where the author visited: Denmark, Sweden, Finland, Norway, and Iceland.

While much historic church architecture exists in the Nordic countries[3], a number of church buildings and chapels have still been built in modern and contemporary times, Lutherans[4] are dominant in the Nordic countries and their expressions of architecture give impressions of freedom. It looks like the attitudes and atmospheres of Lutheranism, which are not too concerned about the authority and tradition, as well as its functional basis and usage as a place for local communities are leading to generate and accept free expressions.

Such architecture, of course, can be seen apart from Lutheran churches or Nordic countries. More church architecture with these free expressions, however, commonly exists in the area compared with the countries with a strong Catholic character. Furthermore, there is much high-quality architecture in the modern churches of Nordic countries, which spontaneously fit in with the local climate; are cherished and used by the believers and visitors while maintaining historical continuity; and give us a realization that they provide luxuriance, beauty, and joy in everyday life. Although being a special type of building, the church architecture provides us many hints for thinking about "the way that architecture should be" in the modern age where new buildings are constructed and consumed one after another.

Most of the church buildings scattered around in various places have the atmosphere and characteristics that are common in the architecture of the Nordic countries, such as a humanity, gentleness, and calmness. Yet the different expressions in the buildings are reflections of the various climates, landscapes, lifestyles and conceptions of nature in each country or area; the attitudes of the churches; and the identities of the architects.

An appearance in an idyllic scene, an attitude of facing a harsh environment, a place created for confronting death and life, a mystique found in darkness, a space filled with white light, an attitude of living in good harmony with natural elements such as forests and water, and an un-church-like free taste; I hope readers will enjoy such commonalities and diversities of the examples in this book.

When visiting churches in the northland, immersing oneself in a quiet space with beautiful light, and spending time while sensing the ever-changing light and nature outside, one will be enveloped by this happy time, as if salvaged from the busy, era of abundance of today. I cannot help thinking that such experiences also become a trigger for reviewing our life in some way.

If readers are given a trigger by this book and can experience the beautiful light and spaces in the church buildings, and perhaps ruminate over various things, it will be more than pleasurable for the author.

Note 1) "Nordic" or the "Nordic countries" includes four countries (Denmark, Sweden, Finland, and Norway), plus the Baltic States, British Isles, and Iceland. However, the former four countries, or five countries if additionally including Iceland, are commonly referred to as Nordic countries. The "Nordic countries" in this book mean these five countries. Additionally, as in the term "Scandinavian design", the Nordic countries are sometimes referred to as "Scandinavia". In this case, Scandinavia includes three countries located on the Scandinavian Peninsula (Denmark, Sweden, and Norway), but is often confused with the Nordic countries and used to include other countries.

2) Here are some notes on the terms and target architecture in this book.

This book mainly includes Christ Churches and many of these are Lutheran Churches3).

A "church" refers to body of Christians, taken as a whole, and a building used for Christian religious worship service. In this book a church means the latter.

This book also contains a chapel, a place of prayer and worship that is usually attached to a larger religious institution and a monastery, a living place for monastics.

In this book, target architecture, consisting of church, chapel, or monastery, as a whole is called a "church" and each target is described with a concrete name.

3) The description below by Daisuke Ito helps in understanding the full picture of old church architecture in the Nordic countries:

"Churches obviously began as a foreign culture in the Northern countries, with the arrival of European styles into major Nordic cities. At the next phase, they had rooted down to the small local villages to reinforce the religious faith. Depending on the route of importation, the introduced style for cathedral construction could be a German style, or French style (or even Russian style) in the Nordic countries. Although coexistence of styles from various countries was an interesting phenomenon in the Nordic countries, it might be said that they were not truly entrenched. Whereas the small churches that infiltrated and indigenized in the villages could not be simply categorized into a "Nordic style", they were rooted with their unique appearances in the indigenous climate of individual Nordic areas." (Daisuke Ito, 2010, Illustration of Architectural Heritages in Nordic Countries: Culture Fostered by Cities and Nature, Kawase Shobo Shinsha Publishers). In his book, he provided examples of these small churches, such as wooden stave churches in Norway, brick or stone construction churches with white stairs-like gables in Denmark, granite construction medieval churches in Finland and Sweden, and modern wooden churches in Finland.

4) Freedom of religion is recognized in the Nordic countries today, yet Lutherans are dominant, as described earlier. The Evangelical Lutheran Church was the state religion of Sweden up until 2000, and of Norway up until 2012, and still is in Iceland, Denmark, and Finland (as of 2017).

Denmark
デンマーク

Bagsvaerd Church
Jørn Utzon, 1976, Bagsvaerd, near Copenhagen

バウスヴェア教会 |ヨーン・ウッツォン| 1976 |バウスヴェア、コペンハーゲン近郊

シドニー・オペラハウスの設計で著名な建築家・ウッツォンによる教会。プレファブの工場のような外観とは対照的に豊かな内部空間が展開する。矩形の全体形の中に、礼拝堂およびサービス諸室等が中庭と共に配置され、それらをつなぐ回廊が巡る。回廊には透明ガラスの屋根がかかり青空とつながるが、礼拝堂へ足を踏み入れると、雲の中に迷い込んだかのような感覚になる。白く塗装されたコンクリートによる有機的な形態の天井が頭上を覆い、見えない位置の開口部から侵入した光が、粗い天井面に拡散反射しながら頭上より舞い降り、礼拝堂全体を白い光で満たす。

A church designed by the architect famous for the designing the Sydney Opera House. In contrast to the exterior appearance resembling a prefabricated factory, various interior spaces are developed. The church space, service room, and other rooms are arranged together around a courtyard in the overall rectangular volume and connected via corridors. The corridors are topped with transparent glass roofs and connected to blue sky. Once stepping into the church space, one would feel as if wandering into a cloud. The organically shaped roof made with white-painted concrete covers overhead. Light enters from invisible openings, is diffusely reflected on the rough ceiling, showers down from above, and fills the entire church space with white light.

1. 礼拝堂　側方 (p012)
2. 西側外観
3. 南側外観
4. 回廊

1. Side of the church space (p012)
2. Exterior appearance of the westside
3. Exterior appearance of the southside
4. Corridor

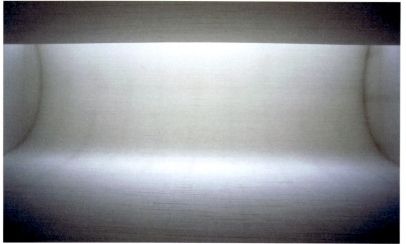

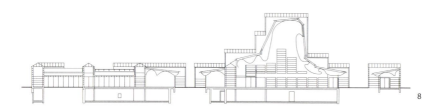

5. 礼拝堂　天井見上げ
6. 直接は見えない位置にあるハイサイドライト
7. 祭壇方向正面
8. 断面図
9. 平面図

5. Church space ceiling viewed from below
6. Clerestory windows hidden from direct view
7. View towards the front side of the altar
8. Sectional plan
9. Floor plan

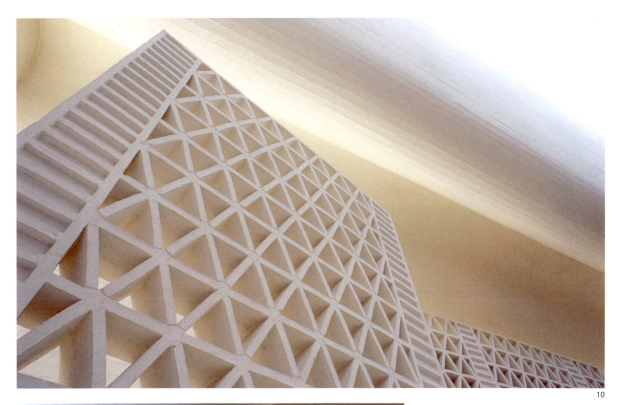

10. 祭壇部見上げ
11. 祭壇部　白い孔あき煉瓦の間仕切り壁

10. Altar viewed from below
11. Partition wall of the altar, made with white perforated bricks

Grundtvigs Church
P.V.Jensen Klint, Kaare Klint, 1940, Copenhagen

グルントヴィ教会 | PV イェンセン、コーレ・クリント | 1940 | コペンハーゲン

デンマークの国づくりに大きな功績を残したグルントヴィ牧師（1783-1872）を記念した教会で、教会周辺の集合住宅なども併せて設計・建設された。ひときわ際だつパイプオルガンのような外観は、デンマークの伝統的な教会が持つ破風屋根の表現とも言われる。内部空間では、ゴシック大聖堂の持つ垂直性や崇高な光を明るい色彩の煉瓦によってシンプルに表現。金色の光と静粛が堂内を満たす。イェンセン・クリントの死後、椅子デザイナーとして著名な息子のコーア・クリントが設計を引き継ぎ完成させた。

A church built to memorialize pastor N. F. S. Grundtvig (1783-1872), who performed an important role in the nation-building of Denmark. The housing complex and other buildings near the church were designed and constructed together. The eye-catching exterior appearance, resembling a pipe organ, is said to be expressionism, or an expression of the gabled roofs of traditional Danish churches. In the interior spaces, the vertical nature and noble light of Gothic cathedrals are simply expressed by light colored bricks. Golden light and silence fill the interior. After the death of architect P.V. Jensen Klint, his son, Kaare Klint, who was a well-known chair designer, took over the design and completion.

1. 教会と周囲の集合住宅等
2. ファサード見上げ
3. 教会内部
4. 平面図
5. 断面図
6. 祭壇方向正面（p017）

1. Church and surrounding housing complexes
2. Façade viewed from below
3. Church interior viewed facing the front of the altar
4. Floor plan
5. Sectional plan
6. Church interior viewed facing the front of the altar (p017)

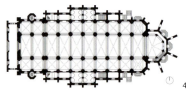
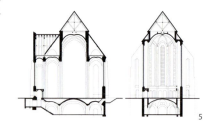

Islev Church

Inger & Johannes Exner, 1970, Rødovre, near Copenhagen

イスレブ教会

| インガー & ヨハネス・エクスナー | 1970 | ロツオウレ、コペンハーゲン近郊

デンマークで教会建築を数多く手がけている建築家夫妻による作品。低層部でコの字型に囲われた中庭に、大きさの異なる三つのヴォリュームが連続する。その一番大きなヴォリュームを持つ空間が、神秘的な暗さが支配する礼拝堂だ。粗い煉瓦壁で囲われた正方形の空間の上部には、木製トラスをもつ天井が架かるが、天井と壁の隙間から入射した太陽光が、粗い煉瓦壁をグラデーションを伴って美しく伝い降りる。そしてそれとは対照的に、足下の横長の開口部からの水平方向の光が床面を明るく照らす。

A church designed by an architect couple, who have made a number of church buildings in Denmark. Three different sized volumes are continuously arranged at the courtyard, surrounded by a U-shaped low-rise building. The space with the largest volume is the church, dominated by mysterious darkness. A ceiling with wooden trusses tops the square space surrounded by rough brick walls. Sunlight penetrating through the gaps between the ceiling and the walls gorgeously descends along the rough brick walls, creating a gradation of light. In contrast, the floor is brightly lit by horizontal light from the horizontally stretched openings at the bottom of the walls.

1. 礼拝堂　木製トラスの天井見上げ
2. 礼拝堂　足下から侵入する光
3. 中庭および連続する３つのヴォリューム
4. 断面図
5. 平面図
6. 礼拝堂　粗い壁面を伝う光 (p019)

1. Ceiling with wooden trusses viewed from below
2. Light penetrating right above the floor
3. Courtyard and continuous three volumes
4. Sectional plan
5. Floor plan
6. Light on a rough wall of the church (p019)

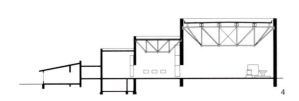
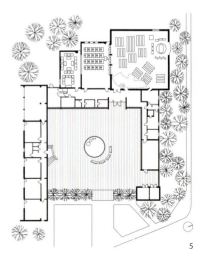

Gug Church
Inger & Johannes Exner, 1972, Aalborg

グウ教会 ｜インガー & ヨハネス・エクスナー｜ 1972 ｜オールボー

斜めのパターンが刻まれたコンクリート打ち放しのボックスが連続する外観。礼拝堂内部は、床が高さを変えながら大きさの異なる空間が連続する。それら空間のつなぎ目には、上部と側部の透明ガラススリットによって光のカーテンが舞い降り、空間移行のシークエンスと空間の連なりを豊かにする。礼拝堂内には多数の裸電球がさまざまな高さで吊り下げられており、光を受けたその吊りワイヤーとともに、その姿はさながら光の雨のようだ。壁面のコンクリート打ち放しには、化粧ナットが加えられることで、パネル張りのような興味深い表情を生み出している。

The exterior appearance with continuation of as-cast concrete boxes with an engraved diagonal pattern. Inside of the church, various sized spaces and different floor heights are continuously placed. Where the spaces join, a curtain of light is formed by transparent glass slits on the top and sides, enhancing the sequence of spatial transitions and continuation of spaces. Numerous naked light bulbs are hung at various heights in the church. Combined with the sunlit wires for hanging, the bulbs create a scene of raining light. By adding face nuts on the as-cast concrete wall surfaces, an interesting expression is formed, as if paneled walls.

1. 祭壇より礼拝堂後方を望む (p020)
2. 化粧ナットのついたコンクリート壁面
3. 外観
4. スリット見上げ
5. 断面図
6. 平面図

1. Rear view of the church from the altar (p020)
2. Concrete wall with face nuts
3. Exterior appearance
4. Slit viewed from below
5. Sectional plan
6. Floor plan

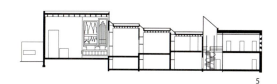
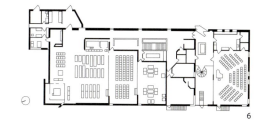

Enghøj Church
Henning Larsen, 1994, Randers

エンホイ教会 ｜ヘニング・ラーセン｜ 1994 ｜ラナース

丘の上に建つV字形の外観が特徴的な教会。内部において、そのV字形は木製の天井によって表現される。天井と壁面の隙間から自然光が舞い降り、天井全体を美しく浮かび上がらせる様は圧巻だ。正方形の小窓が規則的に設けられたコンクリート打ち放しの壁面には、彫りの深いパネルの目地とセパレーターの丸孔により強い陰影が刻印される。祭壇の後ろには一枚の壁が付加され、その上方および左右から入射する光によって、祭壇後部が額縁のように輝き神々しさを演出している。

A church building with characteristic V-shaped exterior, built on top of a hill. The V-shape is expressed inside of the building as a wooden ceiling. It is overwhelming to see natural light showering through gaps between the ceiling and walls, and that beautifully illuminates the entire ceiling. On the as-cast concrete with regularly arranged small square windows, deeply carved joints of the panels and round holes of the separator cast deep shadows. Light entering from above and the sides of the additional wall behind the altar illuminate the back of the altar, as if a frame, and creates a celestial scene.

1. 礼拝堂　祭壇方向 (p022)
2. 祭壇
3. 祭壇と背後の壁
4. 外観
5. 平面図
6. 断面図
7. 側面壁と木製天井 (p024-025)
8. 礼拝堂後方を望む (p026)

1. Church interior viewed facing the altar (p022)
2. Altar
3. Altar and the wall behind
4. Exterior appearance
5. Floor plan
6. Sectional plan
7. Side wall and wooden ceiling (p024-025)
8. Back of the church interior (p026)

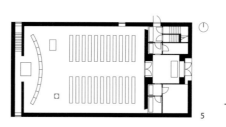

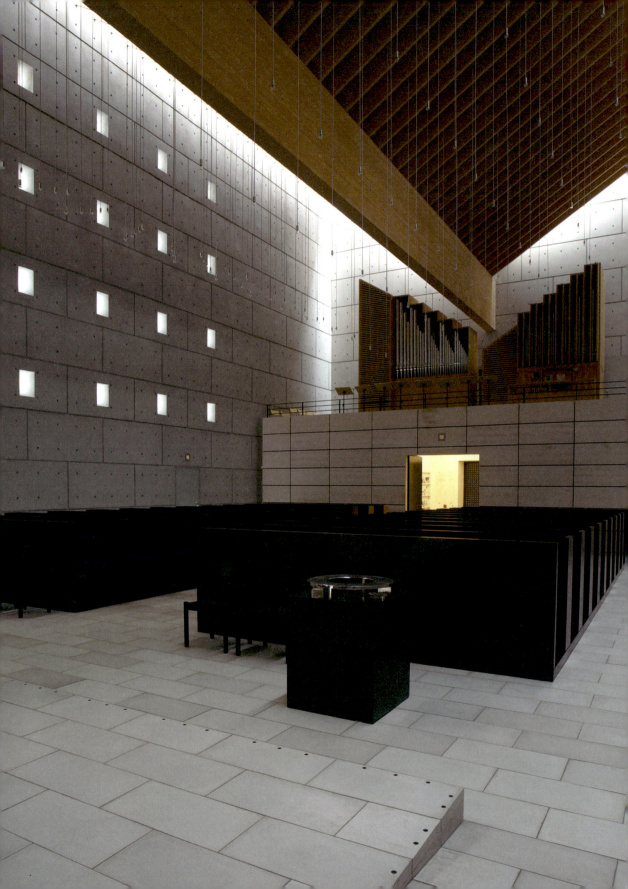

Aarhus Chapel Crematorium
Henning Larsen, 1967, Aarhus

オーフス火葬場の礼拝堂 ｜ヘニング・ラーセン｜ 1967｜オーフス

前例エンホイ教会のＶ字形天井のモチーフは、27年前竣工のオーフス公営墓地内火葬場の礼拝堂で、コンクリート打ち放しによる表現にて試みられていた。その形態は、左右から斜めに降りる板と中央の垂直板の３枚のコンクリート板で構成されるが、そこから導かれる光はエンホイ教会とは大きく異なる。Ｖ字形の器にたまった水が、中央の垂直板によって両サイドに振り分けられるかのように、光が堂内に舞い降りてくる。のちに礼拝堂に隣接するホールの増築が行われたが、その部分は地元オーフスの建築家による。

A motif of the V-shaped ceiling in the Enghøl Church (previous example) was already tried by using as-cast concrete in the Aarhus Chapel Crematorium, completed 27 years earlier at a public cemetery in Aarhus. The form consists of three concrete panels: diagonal panels sloping down from both sides, and a vertical panel at the center. However, light induced from there is much different from the Enghøl Church. As if water stored in a V-shaped container spilling down both sides of the vertical board at the center, light showers down on the room. The adjacent hall, designed by a local architect in Aarhus, was later added next to the chapel.

1. 外観
2. 礼拝堂　後方
3. 増築部へつながる回転扉
4. 断面図
5. 平面図

1. Exterior appearance
2. Back of the chapel
3. Pivoting door to the extension
4. Sectional plan
5. Floor plan

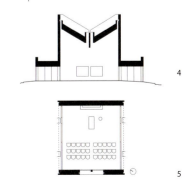

Egedal Church
Fogh&Følner, 1990, kokkedal

1. 南側壁面。銃眼のような窓が並ぶ
2. 外観
3. 平面図
4. 礼拝堂全景 (p029)

1. South side wall. Gunport-like windows are aligned.
2. Exterior appearance
3. Floor plan
4. Full view of the church interior (p029)

エーエダル教会 |フォウ&フェルナー| 1990 |コケダル

森林開拓地に建つこの教会は、中庭を囲むコの字型の平面形を持ち、白煉瓦のストライプが入った赤い煉瓦壁によるヴォリュームが、羽を広げたように森を背に浮かび上がる。礼拝堂内部は、白い壁と木の天井、暖色系の煉瓦タイルなどより構成され、正面右手の足下から天井までのスリットとそこからの光で垂直性が高められる。片流れの屋根形状に合わせて、木製の天井は南側に向かって緩やかなカーブを描きながら上方へと登る。

Built in a forest clearing, the church has a U-shaped plan surrounding a courtyard. The red-brick walled volume with white brick stripes stands out as if it were spreading its wing in front of the forest. The interior of the church consists of white walls, a wooden ceiling, warm-colored brick tiles, etc. Slits on the front right that stretch from the floor to the ceiling, and light coming thorough the slits enhance the vertical feature. In accordance with the shed roof form, the wooden ceiling is gently curved and sloped upward to the south side.

Sankt Clemens Church
Inger & Johannes Exner, Knud Erik Larsen, 1963, Randers

1

聖クレメンス教会 ｜インガー＆ヨハネス・エクスナー、クヌツ・エーリク・ラーセン｜1963｜ラナース

眺望のよい南に開けた斜面地に建つ教会。アプローチは斜面とは反対の車道側からであるが、礼拝堂は斜面に向かって幅が広がり、先端部は三角形状に突き出す。その先端の壁は、暖色の煉瓦タイル張りの壁柱とガラススリットの単純な連続であるが、光の方向や強さ、直射光、曇天光、樹木に反射して色付けられた光など、その時々で異なる入射光が、豊かな表情を礼拝堂に運び込む。後方の木による架構やパイプオルガンなども丁寧なデザインがなされている。

The church stands on a south-facing, open slope with a scenic view. Approached from the roadside (opposite from the slope), the church has a wider width towards the slope, with its triangular-shaped tip projecting. The tip wall consists of a simple continuation of warm-colored brick tiled wall pillars and glass slits; however, ever-changing incoming light (e.g., light with various light directions and intensity, direct light, light of a cloudy day, and colored light reflected on trees) brings plentiful expressions into the church. The wooden framework and pipe organ at the back of the church were also carefully designed.

1. 礼拝堂　午前中のスリット状の光
2. アプローチ側外観
3. 側面
4. 斜面下から見上げる
5. 断面図
6. 平面図

1. Church lit by morning light through the slits
2. Exterior appearance from the approach side
3. Side view
4. Church view from the lower side of the slope
5. Sectional plan
6. Floor plan

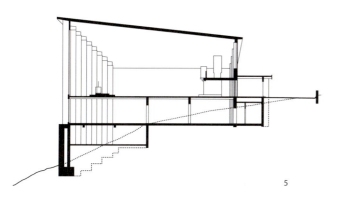
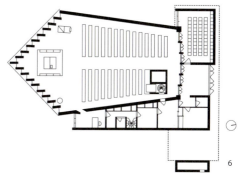

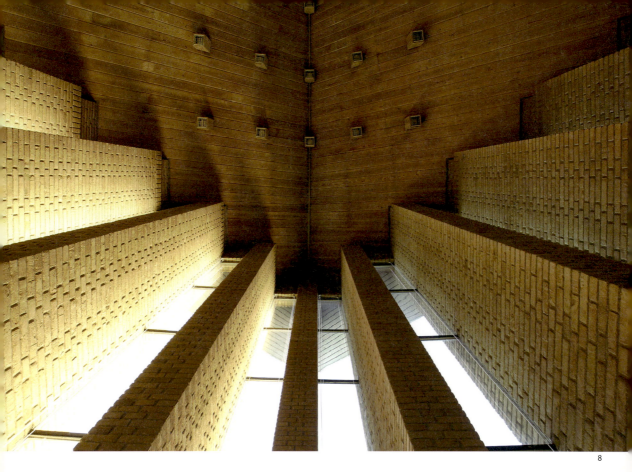

7. 強い光を受けた正面壁（p032）
8. 天井見上げ
9. 祭壇
10. 礼拝堂後方　木の架構とパイプオルガン

7. Front wall lit by strong sunlight (p032)
8. Ceiling viewed from below
9. Altar
10. Wooden framework and pipe organ at the back of the church

Country view of Lolland
ローランド島の田園風景

Tornbjerg Church
Fogh&Følner, 1994, Odense

トーンビア教会　| フォウ&フェルナー | 1994 | オーデンセ

緩やかな曲面屋根を持つ異なるヴォリュームが重なり合いながらこの教会は構成されている。そのルーフスケープは、広がりのある景観の中で優雅さを醸し出している。裏側の外壁は煉瓦だが、石灰を塗りこんだものと白塗りしたものを組み合わせることで、落ち着きある風合いを保ちながら、単調さを回避し人間的なスケール感を生み出すことに成功している。礼拝堂内部は、同設計者によるエーエダル教会（p028）と類似し、足下から天井までのスリットと小窓によって、美しい光の空間が現出している。

The church building is structured by overlapping different volumes with a gently curved roof. The roofscape adds elegance to the open scenery of the surroundings. The exterior wall at the back is made of brick; however, by combining lime coated bricks and white painted bricks, monotony is successfully avoided while retaining a sedate texture, as well as creating a sense of human scale. The interior of the church is similar to Egedal Church (p.) designed by the same architect. A beautiful light space is realized by the slits extending from the floor to the ceiling, and small windows.

1. 礼拝堂（p036）
2. 礼拝堂　祭壇横側壁
3. エントランス周り
4. 裏側の外壁詳細
5. 正面　外観
6. 断面図
7. 平面図

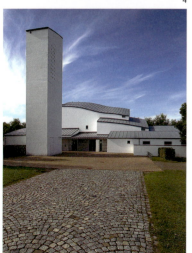

1. Chapel (p036)
2. Wall beside the altar in the church
3. Around the entrance
4. Detail of the exterior wall at the back
5. Exterior appearance of the front
6. Sectional plan
7. Floor plan

Church of the Resurrection
Inger & Johannes Exner, 1984, Albertslund, near Copenhagen

1. 祭壇から（p038）
2. 外観
3. 天井見上げ
4. 光を受けた壁
5. 断面図
6. 平面図

1. View from the altar (p038)
2. Exterior appearance
3. Sunlit wall
4. Ceiling viewed from below
5. Sectional plan
6. Floor plan

復活教会　｜インガー＆ヨハネス・エクスナー｜1984｜アルベアツルン、コペンハーゲン近郊

コペンハーゲン近郊の教会。礼拝堂は、8枚の壁を隙間に透明ガラススリットを設けながら形成した八角形をしている。その壁は、石灰塗りの煉瓦壁を基調に、ピンク色の煉瓦によって、微妙な凹凸と色彩の変化がつけられている。それらの壁は、時刻によって異なる方向からの光を受け止め、時の変化とともに光が礼拝堂の空間を巡り、その変動を空間的に増幅させる。デンマークの建築は日本建築の影響を多分に受けたと言われるが、この教会のホールなどの部分にはその影響が色濃く見られる。

The church is located near Copenhagen. The octagonal shaped church space is formed by eight walls with transparent glass slits in between. The walls are basically made with lime coated bricks, and pink bricks are used to add subtle unevenness and different shades of color. Light from different directions depending on the time of day shines on the walls, and the light passes through the church spaces over time, enhancing the transition of light within the spaces. It is said that Danish architecture was greatly influenced by Japanese architecture, and the strong influence can be found in the hall and other parts of this church.

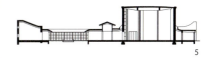

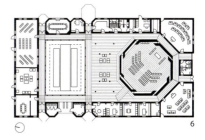

7. 壁とスリット見上げ（p040）　　7. View of the wall and slits from below (p040)
8. 中庭周り　　　　　　　　　　　8. Around the courtyard
9. ホール　　　　　　　　　　　　9. Hall

Dybkær Church
Regnbuen Arkitekter, 2010, Silkeborg

1. 礼拝堂　祭壇方向
2. 側廊から身廊方向
3. 外観
4. 平面図
5. 十字架と白い壁面 (p043)

1. Church viewed facing the altar
2. Nave viewed from the aisle
3. Exterior appearance
4. Floor plan
5. The cross and white wall (p043)

デュブケア教会 | ラインブーエン建築設計事務所 | 2010 | シルケボー

中庭を中心に矩形で構成された教会。赤茶系のストライプがはいった落ち着きのある煉瓦壁の外観と白い内部空間という、外と内の色彩の関係性はデンマークではよく見られる手法だ。礼拝堂の左右の白い煉瓦壁には、音響効果のために不揃いの細長い孔があけられており、微妙な振動が感じられるような不思議な視覚的効果を与える。正面壁のトップライトと右手のスリット窓に加えて、十字架背後の隅部の光など、各所に設けられた窓はそれぞれ絶妙な光の効果をもたらし、空間全体に調和と緊張感をもたらしている。

The rectangular church building built around a courtyard. The sedate exterior appearance of brick walls with reddish brown stripes and the white interior spaces: such a relationship of interior and exterior colors is often found in Denmark. On the white brick walls on both sides of the church space, uneven narrow holes are made for acoustic effect, providing an intriguing visual effect that apparently enables sensation of subtle vibrations. In addition to the skylight over the front wall and the slit window on the right, windows at various locations (such as at the lower corner behind the cross) give perfect lighting effects, and create harmony and a sense of tension in the entire space.

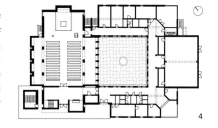

Antvorskov Church
Regnbuen Arkitekter, 2005, Slagelse

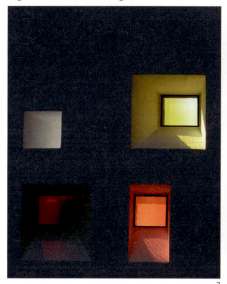

アントヴォスコウ教会

| ラインブーエンデュブ建築設計事務所 | 2005 | スラーエルセ |

デュブケア教会と同じ設計者の作品。小高い敷地の芝生の広がりの中で落ち着いた外観を呈す教会。茶系の外壁とは対照的に、礼拝堂の内部は白い煉瓦壁で構成される色彩の関係性はこの教会でも同様だ。白く塗装された木製の天井が、音響効果を考慮し緩やかな波を描きながら祭壇方向へと上昇する。正面壁の幅いっぱいにはスリット状のトップライトが設けられ、そこからの光が正面壁を浮かび上がらせるが、中央の窪んだ部分が大きな光の変化を生み出している。直射光とうっすらとした反射光の筋のクロスも美しい。正面向かって右手の白い壁柱による列柱空間や、異なる色彩を奏でる窓群も印象的だ。

Designed by the same architect as the Dybkær church. The sedate appearing church stands on a wide spread of lawn on a low hill site. The relationship of the colors (brownish exterior walls and contrasting white brick walls in the church) is also seen in this church. The white-painted wooden ceiling gently waves and rises towards the altar, in consideration of an acoustic effect. A slit-shaped skylight covers the entire width of the front wall and the light from it illuminates the front wall, while the recessed part at the center adds dynamic variation in light. Crossings of direct sunlight and faint reflected light are also beautiful. The colonnaded space with white wall pillars on the front right and the group of windows with different colors also give a strong impression.

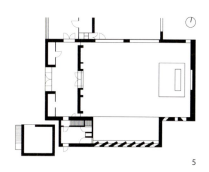

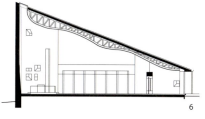

1. 礼拝堂　祭壇方向 (p044)
2. 色彩を与える窓群
3. 白い列柱空間
4. 列柱部分の外観
5. 平面図
6. 断面図
7. 祭壇上部見上げ (p046-047)

1. Church viewed facing the altar (p044)
2. Group of windows add color
3. White colonnaded space
4. Exterior appearance of the colonnaded space
5. Floor plan
6. Sectional plan
7. View of upper altar from below (p046-047)

Sweden

スウェーデン

The Woodland Cemetery
Erik Gunnar Asplund, 1940, Stockholm

2

3

森の火葬場 | グンナール・アスプルンド | 1940 | ストックホルム

十字架を目標に低い壁に導かれ、緩やかな坂道をアプローチするその先には、人は終に空と森へ還るとのメッセージが込められている。この劇的なシークエンス体験は、どの季節時刻天候に訪れても感動的だ。世界遺産登録の火葬場と礼拝堂群。十字架を過ぎ左手のロッジアを進む中、屋根に孔いた開口部分では彫刻の動きと共に意識は空へと向けられる。その後、主礼拝堂に導かれるが、堂内の床には緩い勾配がつけられており、その先の丸みをもった正面の壁面が意識を受け止める。最後の別れを告げ、礼拝堂を出た先には緩やかにのぼる大地の先に瞑想の丘がある。

Beyond the gently sloped approach, guided by short walls and the cross as a landmark, there is a message: people ultimately return to the sky and forest. This dramatic sequential experience is always impressive, regardless of season, time, and weather. The crematorium and chapels are named a UNESCO World Heritage Site. When going through the loggia on the left side after passing the cross, one's consciousness is oriented to the sky under the opening in the roof, led by the form of the sculpture. Continuing to chapel of the holly Cross, where the floor is gently sloped, one's consciousness is caught by the rounded front wall. The meditation hill is behind a gentle slope at the back of the chapel, where people bid farewell to the departed.

1. 雪が残る春のアプローチ (p050-051)
2. 夏のアプローチ
3. 池越しの瞑想の丘
4. 全体配置図
5. ロッジア
6. ロッジアから主礼拝堂方向
7. ロッジア 見上げ 彫刻はヨーン・ルンドクヴィスト（John Lundqvist）作

1. Snow-covered approach in spring (p050-051)
2. Approach in summer
3. Meditation hill behind a pond
4. Overall layout
5. Loggia
6. Chapel of the holly Cross viewed from the loggia
7. Loggia viewed from below and the sculpture by John Lundqvist

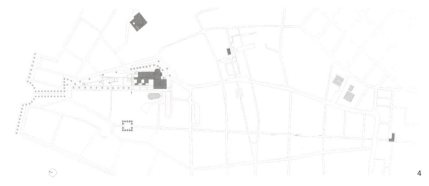

4

5

6

7

8. 主礼拝堂（p054-055）
9. 主礼拝堂　祭壇より（p056）
10. 断面図
11. 平面図
12. 納骨の庭を裏から望む
13. 納骨の庭
14. 葬礼の様子

8. Main chapel (p054-055)
9. Main chapel viewed from the altar (p056)
10. Sectional plan
11. Floor plan
12. Orm Garden viewd from the backside
13. Orm Garden
14. Funeral tites

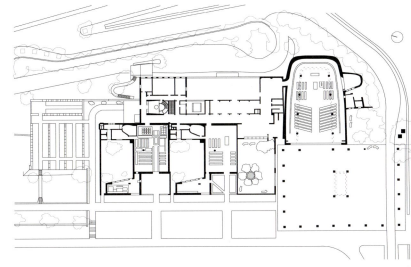

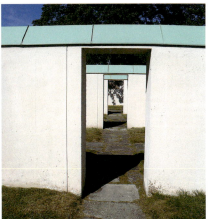

The Woodland Chapel
Erik Gunnar Asplund, 1940 Stockholm

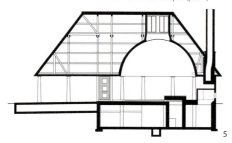

森の礼拝堂 ｜グンナール・アスプルンド｜1940｜ストックホルム

松の林の中、白い門をくぐると小道の先に杮葺き屋根の小さな礼拝堂が静かに佇んでいる。トスカーナ様式の柱によるポルティコは、森から内部空間への移行を段階的に行い、鋳鉄の扉まで導いてくれる。そしてその植物文様の扉の向こうは、ドーム空間に覆われたほんのりと明るい空間が透けて見える。堂内に入り、ドーム空間の周囲を巡る列柱による結界を超えると、森から水平方向に進んだシークエンスは、垂直方向の空へと昇り完結する。

A small, wood-shingled roof chapel quietly stands down a path beyond a white gate in a pine tree woodland. The gradual transition from the woodland to the interior space is facilitated by a portico with Tuscan style pillars, which leads to a cast-iron door with a plant pattern. A dimly lit space covered by a dome is visible through the door. By entering the chapel and passing the colonnaded boundary enclosing the dome, the horizontal sequence from the woodland is completed as it vertically extends up to the sky.

1. ポルティコから振り返る
2. 門
3. アプローチ路から礼拝堂正面
4. 鋳鉄の扉
5. 断面図
6. 平面図
7. 礼拝堂内（p059）

1. View looking back from the portico
2. Gate
3. Front view of the chapel from the approach
4. Cast-iron door
5. Sectional plan
6. Floor plan
7. Interior of the chapel (p059)

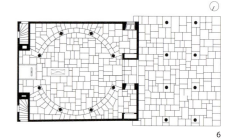

Chapel of the Resurrection
Sigurd Lewerentz, 1925, Stockholm

復活礼拝堂 |シーグルド・レヴェレンツ| 1925 |ストックホルム

森の火葬場の計画は、アスプルンドと同時代の建築家レヴェレンツとの共同で始まり、1935年よりアスプルンド単独になり、現在の全体計画と礼拝堂が完成している。そのレヴェレンツが1925年に敷地内に設計した新古典主義の礼拝堂である。左右対称を崩したポルティコや窓の配置と独特のプロポーションが外観の特徴だ。外部において偏心した位置にある唯一の窓から射し込む光は、彩度を落とした虚ろな灰色の内部空間に、生気を与える重要な役割を果たしている。

Planning of the Woodland Crematory was begun by Asplund and an architect of the same age, Lewerentz, but then Asplund worked alone after 1935 and completed the overall plan and the chapel existing today. This neoclassical chapel built within the site was designed by Lewerentz in 1925. The asymmetric arrangement of a portico and windows as well as unique proportions are characteristics of the exterior. The only window at an uncentered location on the exterior wall provides light, which plays a crucial role in providing vital spirit into the dull colored, gray, and empty interior space.

1. 礼拝堂　祭壇方向 (p061)
2. 壁に投影された光と影
3. 外観
4. 断面図
5. 平面図

1. Chapel viewed facing the altar (p061)
2. Light and shadow casted on a wall
3. Exterior appearance
4. Sectional plan
5. Floor plan

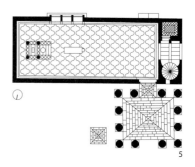

6. 敷地内に 2013 年に新しく出来た火葬施設の外観。設計は、ヨハンセルシング（p084）「森の中の石 stone in the forest」と呼ばれる。
 The New Crematorium, The Woodland Cemetery/ Johan Celsing Arkitektkontor
7. 同　キャノピーから森を見返し
8. 同　キャノピーから側方
9. 火葬施設
10. 森の火葬場内　墓地（p063）

6. The exterior appearance of a crematorium called "A Stone in the Forest", newly built in 2013 within the site. Designed by Johan Celsing Arkitektkontor (p084).
7. View of the forest from the canopy of the crematorium
8. Side view from the canopy of the crematorium
9. Crematorium
10. Burying ground in the Woodland Cemetery (p063)

11. 雪のつもる瞑想の丘
12. 白夜と月光 (p065)

11. Snow-covered meditation hill
12. Moonlight in white night (p065)

Chapels of St. Knut and St. Gertrud
Sigurd Lewerentz, 1943, 1955, Malmö

2　　3　　4

聖クヌット・聖ゲアトルド礼拝堂

| シーグルド・レヴェレンツ | 1943, 1955 | マルメ

新古典主義の復活礼拝堂から20年近くを経て設計された火葬施設に併設した対になる2つの礼拝堂。その後のレヴェレンツの独特な作風へとつながる作品だ。スウェーデン南部の大都市マルメの西部公営墓地内にある。二つの礼拝堂の入口には、直線的な柱と木組み屋根によるポーティコが設けられ、独特の雰囲気を作り出している。堂内では、大理石の砕片が埋め込まれた黄色い煉瓦壁、テラゾーの床、松材の薄片による仕上げなどが、厳粛で静けさに満ちる空間に、砕かれた光を編み込んでいる。

5

Designed about 20 years after the neoclassical Chapel of Resnrrection. The two paired chapels, built next to a crematorium, precede the unique style in later works of Lewerentz. The chapels are located in the western public cemetery in the major city of Malmö in southern Sweden. The portico at the entrance of each chapel consists of rectilinear pillars and a wooden roof, creating a unique atmosphere. In the quiet, solemn interior space of the chapel, fragmented light is incorporated by the yellow brick wall with embedded marble chips, terrazzo floor, finish of thin pine wood pieces, etc.

1. 礼拝堂入口（p066）
2. ポルティコ見上げ
3. 聖ゲアドルド礼拝堂　内部
4. 聖クヌット礼拝堂　控え室
5. 聖クヌット礼拝堂　控え室外観
6. 断面図
7. 平面図

1. Eentrance of Chapel (p066)
2. Portico
3. Chapel of St. Gertrud
4. Chapet of St. knut Waiting room
5. Exterior of the waiting room
6. Sectional plan
7. Floor plan

 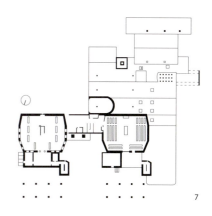

6　　7

St. Mark's Church
Sigurd Lewerentz, 1960, Stockholm

聖マーク教会 |シーグルド・レヴェレンツ| 1960 |ストックホルム

レヴェンレンツの後期名作の一つである聖マーク教会は森の火葬場からほど近い白樺の森の中に建つ。茶系統の焼き煉瓦と灰色のモルタルによる落ち着いた外観を呈す教会は、抑えられたヴォリュームも相俟って周囲に溶け合って存在する。外壁と同じ素材で構成された礼拝堂内部では、薄暗さの中、小さな開口部からの抑制された光が連続するヴォールト天井などをかすかに浮かび上がらせる。礼拝堂に隣接する集会室等の施設棟は、緩やかなヴォールト屋根が連続する人間的スケールの建物だ。その前には、かつてこの敷地が沼地であったことを思い起こさせる池と噴水がある。

One of Lewerentz's masterpieces in his later years, St. Mark's Church stands in a white birch forest near the Woodland Crematory. The church merges into the surroundings, due to its sedate appearance of brownish burnt bricks and gray mortar, combined with the suppressed volume. The underlit interior of the church consists of the same materials as the exterior. Limited light through small openings dimly illuminates the continuous vaulted ceiling. Continuous, gently vaulted roofs top the human-scaled, adjacent facility building, including a meeting room. A pond and fountain in front of the building remind us of the original swampy landscape.

1. 施設棟前の池と噴水
2. 教会 外観
3. 礼拝堂内部 煉瓦のヴォールト天井
4. 断面図
5. 平面図
6. 礼拝堂内部 祭壇方向（p069）

1. Pond and fountain in front of the facility building
2. Exterior of the church
3. Vaulted brick ceiling in the church
4. Sectional plan
5. Floor plan
6. Church viewed facing the altar (p069)

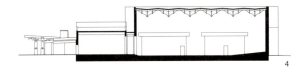

Church of St. Peter
Sigurd Lewerentz, 1966, Klippan

聖ペーター教会 │シーグルド・レヴェレンツ│ 1966 │クリッパン

この教会では、クラフトマンとの良き協働から生まれた粗野で中世的な黒い煉瓦が、外壁、内壁をはじめ、天井、床、そしてベンチとテーブルなどにまで徹底して用いられることで禁欲的な空間が生み出されている。正方形の平面形をもつ礼拝堂は、神秘的な闇に包まれ、めくれ上がった煉瓦床、鉄骨の架構に支えられた連続ヴォールトの煉瓦天井などが、目が慣れた頃にかすかな光によってようやく認識出来る。外壁に突きつけられたガラスをはじめ、全ての細部にまで完全性が求められている。

Stoic spaces are created in this church by thoroughly using the rustic, medieval black bricks that were made through good cooperative work with craftsmen, for the exterior and interior walls, ceilings, and floors, and even benches and tables. The church space with a square plan is enclosed in mysterious darkness. After eyes are adjusted, a feeble light eventually helps in recognizing a rise of the brick floor, and the continuous brick vaulted ceiling supported by a steel framework. Perfection was pursued in every detail, such as the frameless windows in which the glazing units are directly mounted to the exterior wall.

1. 礼拝堂内部（p070） 煉瓦はスウェーデンのヘルシングボリ産
2. 前室より礼拝堂
3. ヴォールト天井を支持する鉄の架構
4. 外観　突きつけのガラス窓
5. 断面図
6. 平面図

1. Interior of the church. Bricks were made in Helsingborg, Sweden (p070)
2. Church space viewed from the neighor room
3. Steel framework supporting the brick vaulted ceiling
4. Exterior wall with frameless glass windows
5. Sectional plan
6. Floor plan

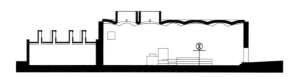
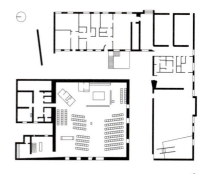

Härlanda Church
Peter Celsing, 1959, Gothenburg

2 3 4

ハーランダ教会 │ペーター・セルシング│ 1959 │ヨーテボリ

アスプルンド、レヴェレンツによる闇の神秘性は、次世代を代表する建築家ペーター・セルシングに引き継がれる。住宅街の小高い場所に、鐘楼、教会棟、執務棟が分棟して建ち、美しいランドスケープを構成する教会。外部も内部も同一の煉瓦壁による礼拝堂には闇が支配し、そこに入射する光が空間に生命力を与える。入口の木格子による光と影のパターンは堂内を動き回る。夕刻、祭壇まで光が射し込む瞬間は感動的だ。壁柱に対面する開口部からの光は壁を照射し、劇的な逆光のシーンを作り出す。

The mystique of darkness by Asplund and Lewerentz was then taken over by Peter Celsing, a representative architect of the following generation. The separate buildings of the church, i.e., a belfry, church, and office building, create a scenic landscape on a slightly elevated site in a residential area. The same brick walls are used for the interior and exterior of the church, which is dominated by darkness. Light entering there gives the space a vital energy. The light and shadow pattern of the wooden latticework at the entrance moves around the church. The moment when the light reaches the altar in the evening is impressive. Light from the opening across the wall pillar illuminates the wall, and creates a dramatic backlit scene.

1. 夕刻の礼拝堂 (p072)
2. 入り口の木格子
3. 教会棟　外観
4. 光を受けた煉瓦壁
5. 断面図
6. 平面図
7. 壁柱の背後からの光 (p074)
8. 教会敷地内のランドスケープ (p075)

1. Church viewed from the altar in the evening (p072)
2. Wooden latticework at the entrance
3. Exterior of the church
4. Sunlit brick wall
5. Sectional plan
6. Floor plan
7. Light from the back of the wall pillar (p074)
8. Landscape within the church site (p075)

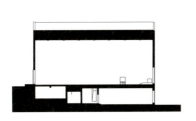

5

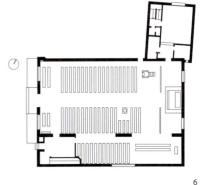

6

073

St. Thomas Church

Peter Celsing, 1959, Vällingby, near Stockholm

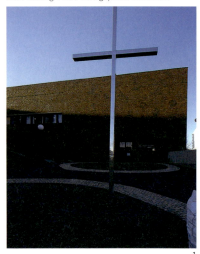

聖トーマス教会

|ペーター・セルシング| 1959 |ヴェリンビュー、ストックホルム近郊|

ストックホルム郊外の駅前からすぐ脇道に入ると、輝くステンレスの十字架と褐色の教会のヴォリュームが現れる。中庭を囲むシンプルな矩形の構成に、鐘楼、階段などの突出物が立体的な変化を付与している。

礼拝堂内部は単純でありながらも絶妙なプロポーションを持ち、天井の目地、梁、縦長の照明器具が空間に直交する方向性を加える。考え抜かれた位置に設けられた窓、格子、水盤などが、それぞれ役割を果たして豊穣なハーモニーを作り上げている。

A shiny stainless steel cross and brownish church volume come into view, when turning into a side street near a station in a suburb of Stockholm. Projections such as a belfry and stairs add three-dimensional variations to the simple rectangular composition around a courtyard.

The interior of the church has a simple yet exquisite proportion. The joints on the ceiling, beams, and tall lighting fixtures insert an orientation perpendicular to the space. The windows, latticework, and water stoup are placed at a location decided after much consideration, and fulfill each role, creating a fertile harmony.

1. 外観
2. 鐘楼　見上げ
3. 十字架と横からの光
4. 水盤と格子窓からの光
5. 断面図
6. 平面図
7. 礼拝堂後方（p077）

1. Exterior appearance
2. Belfry viewed from below
3. Cross lit from the side
4. Water stoup and light from the lattice windows
5. Sectional plan
6. Floor plan
7. Back of the church (p077)

Almtuna Church
Peter Celsing, 1959, Uppsala

1. 中庭から礼拝堂
2. 礼拝堂内部
3. 外観
4. 礼拝堂　後方
5. 断面図
6. 平面図
7. 礼拝堂　祭壇より後方をみる　左手が中庭 (p079)

1. View of the church from the courtyard
2. Interior view of the church facing the altar
3. Exterior appearance
4. Rear of the church
5. Sectional plan
6. Floor plan
7. Back of the church viewed from the altar. The courtyard is on the left side. (p079)

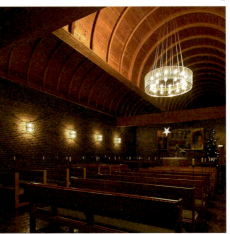

アルムトゥーマ教会 | ペーター・セルシング | 1959 | ウプサラ

北欧で最大級の大聖堂や最古の大学がある、スウェーデン中部の都市ウプサラにある小さな教会。

二つの棟に挟まれた中庭部分は、道路面より一層分持ち上げられ、主要なアプローチは階段を登るところから始まる。煉瓦と木を主材料とし、人間的なスケールで作られたこの教会には、暖かく家庭的な雰囲気が漂う。教会内部は、平行に並ぶ木製の３つのヴォールト天井が空間を優しく包みながら緩やかに分節する。中庭側の木製格子窓からの光は、弱められながら奥まで導かれる。

A small church in the city of Uppsala in central Sweden, where one of the largest cathedrals in the Nordic countries and the oldest university exists.
　The courtyard between two buildings is one level higher than the road surface, where the main approach begins from ascending some stairs. A warm and homey atmosphere can be felt at this church made mainly with bricks and wood in a human scale. Three parallel wooden vaulted ceilings in the church tenderly wrap the space, while loosely articulating it. Light from wooden lattice windows on the courtyard side reaches the back with weakening.

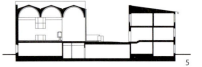

Olaus Petri Church
Peter Celsing, 1959, Stockholm

1

オーラス・ペトリ教会 |ペーター・セルシング| 1959 |ストックホルム

ストックホルム市内にある集合住宅を主用途とした建物に組み込まれた教会。落ち着いた色彩の緩やかにカーブしたヴォリュームを背景に、白く骨太な十字架が映える。プログラム上、全体は単純な複層構成と横長連窓で構成されているが、教会もその基本形を踏襲している。外観からはわかりにくいが、礼拝堂奥の内陣部は二層分の高さを確保し、窓は横長連窓でありながらも高窓としている。白を基調としたシンプルな空間に木の風合いと落ち着いた色彩が調和する。

1. 外観
2. 教会　祭壇方向
3. 教会　後方のハイサイドライト
4. 教会　祭壇より後方
5. 立面図
6. 平面図

1. Exterior appearance
2. Church viewed facing the altar
3. Clerestory windows at the back of the church
4. Back of the church viewed from the altar
5. Elevation plan
6. Floor plan

A church built in a building mainly consisting of housing complexes in Stockholm. A big-boned, white cross stands out in the background of a sedately colored, gently curving volume. Due to the program, the entire building is composed of a simple multilayer composition and horizontally-long ribbon windows, and the church follows this basic style. Although it is hard to see from the exterior, the chancel at the back of the church has a two-story height, and the ribbon windows are made at high locations. The texture of wood and the sedate color are well-matched to the simple space with a basic tone of white.

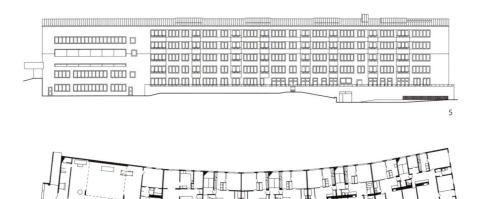

Nacksta Church
Peter Celsing, 1969, Sundsvall

ナクスタ教会 | ペーター・セルシング | 1969 | スンスヴァル

ここまで紹介したセルシングが設計した一連の教会より、10 年ほど後に設計された最後の教会。ノアの方舟をモチーフにしたシンボリックな形態、ダークブルーの外壁などは、煉瓦を主としたシンプルな構成のこれまでの作風とは大きく異なる。

敷地は一層分の高低差があり、礼拝堂へは高い方よりアプローチをする。礼拝堂内部は白を基調とし、木製の天井と架構が全体を引き締める。祭壇に向かって左手の連窓には、フィンが二段に設けられ、光を上方へと跳ね上げる。

The last church designed by Celsing, after about a ten-year interval from the previously introduced churches. The symbolic form with a motif of Noah's Ark and the dark blue exterior walls are significantly different from his previous simple style, mainly consisting of bricks.

 The approach to the church floor is on the higher side of the sloped site, which is elevated in height by one story. The wooden ceiling and framework pepper the overall white-based interior space of the church. The ribbon windows on the left side of the altar have double fins, reflecting light upwards.

1. 教会　祭壇方向 (p082)
2. 窓の二重のフィン
3. 礼拝堂内部
4. 外観
5. 断面図
6. 平面図

1. Church viewed facing the altar (p082)
2. Double fins
3. Church interior
4. Exterior appearance
5. Sectional plan
6. Floor plan

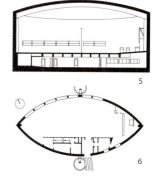

083

Årsta Church
Johan Celsing, 2008, Årsta, near Stockholm

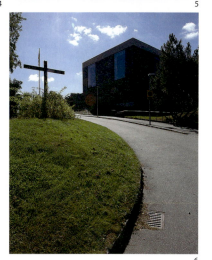

オースタ教会 |ヨハン・セルシング| 2008 |オースタ、ストックホルム近郊

ペーター・セルシングの息子で現代のスウェーデン建築界を代表する建築家ヨハン・セルシング。ストックホルム近郊の町、道路から少し昇った岩場の露出する敷地にこの教会は建つ。礼拝堂は正方形の平面形で、上部に廻る6つの窓は、空と明るさ、そして直射光による動きを礼拝堂に導き、ランダムに配された深い梁は天井に陰影をあたえる。教会全体にわたり、素材の選択から、連続・切り返しの仕方など、煉瓦・タイルの秀逸な扱い方が、シークエンスの展開をより豊かに彩っている。

Johan Celsing, a son of Peter Celsing, is a representative architect of Sweden today. In a suburb of Stockholm, the church stands at a rocky site, elevated from the road. The main church has a square plan, where six high windows introduce the sky, lightness, and movements caused by direct sunlight. The deep beams are randomly placed, adding shadows to the ceiling. The development of the sequence is further garnished by the material choice and superb handling of bricks and tiles, such as the methods of continuing and switching, throughout the church building.

1. エントランスより礼拝堂
2. 礼拝堂　祭壇方向
3. 祭壇
4. 沈黙の礼拝堂への入口
5. 子供用礼拝堂
6. 外観
7. 断面図
8. 平面図

1. Main church viewed from the entrance
2. Main church viewed facing the altar
3. Altar
4. Entrance to the chapel of stillness
5. Children´s chapel
6. Exterior appearance
7. Sectional plan
8. Floor plan

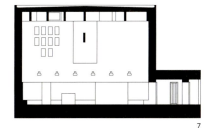 

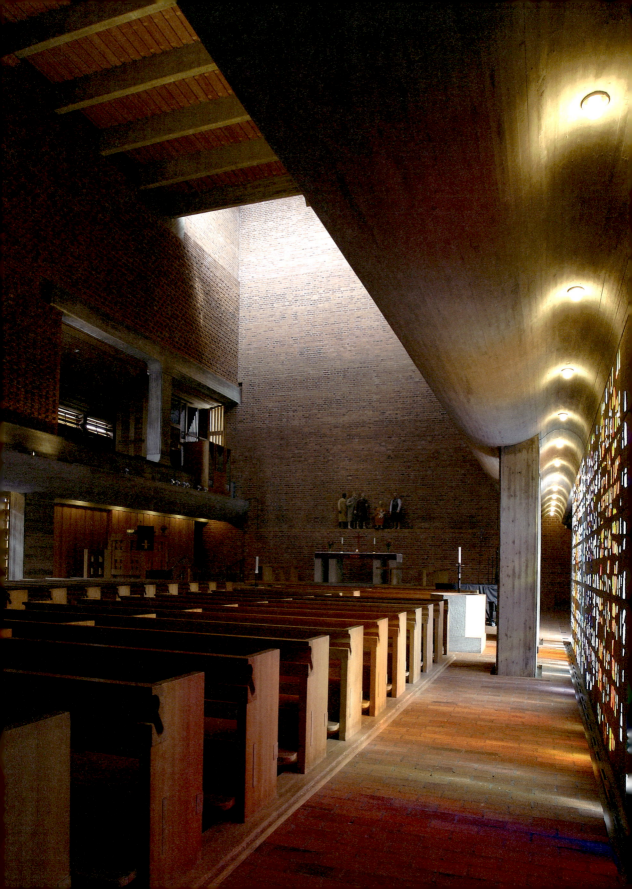

Farsta Församling Söderleds Church
Borgström and Lindroos, 1960, Farsta, near Stockholm

ファースタ・フォサムリン・ソーダレツ教会

| ボリストロム&リンドロース | 1960 | ファースタ、ストックホルム近郊 |

ストックホルム市南部にあるこの教会は、諸施設群からなる低層のL字型の棟と、そこへ角度を微妙にふって配置された大小のホールと中庭を持つ矩形の棟で構成される。内外ともに主要な素材は、赤茶けた煉瓦である。礼拝堂は、高い天井を持つ中央部から、湾曲した天井によって両サイドの低い天井部へと連続するハット状の形態だ。祭壇上部は、さらなる高みから舞い降りる光によって上方を志向する。南側の低い天井部分には、枠の造形が美しいステンドグラスが一面に施されており、色鮮やかな光を堂内に導いている。

Located at the southern part of Stockholm, the church consists of a low-rise, L-shaped facility building, and a rectangular building with small and large halls and a courtyard, which are arranged in a finely adjusted angle. The main material of both the interior and exterior is reddish brown bricks. The church hall is hat-shaped: from the high ceiling at the center, curvy ceilings connect the lower ceilings on both sides. Above the altar, showering light from an even greater height directs attention upward. At the south side with a lower ceiling, stained glass with exquisitely shaped frames cover the entire wall and provide stunning colored light in the church.

1. 礼拝堂　祭壇方向（p086）
2. 礼拝堂　祭壇より後方
3. 礼拝堂　北側の格子窓
4. 外観　後方が礼拝堂
5. 断面図
6. 平面図
7. 礼拝堂中庭側のステンドグラス（p088-089）

1. Church hall viewed facing the altar (p086)
2. Back of the church viewed from the altar
3. Lattice window at the north side of the church
4. Exterior appearance. The church located at the back.
5. Sectional plan
6. Floor plan
7. Stained glass on the courtyard side of the chapel (p088-089)

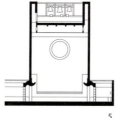

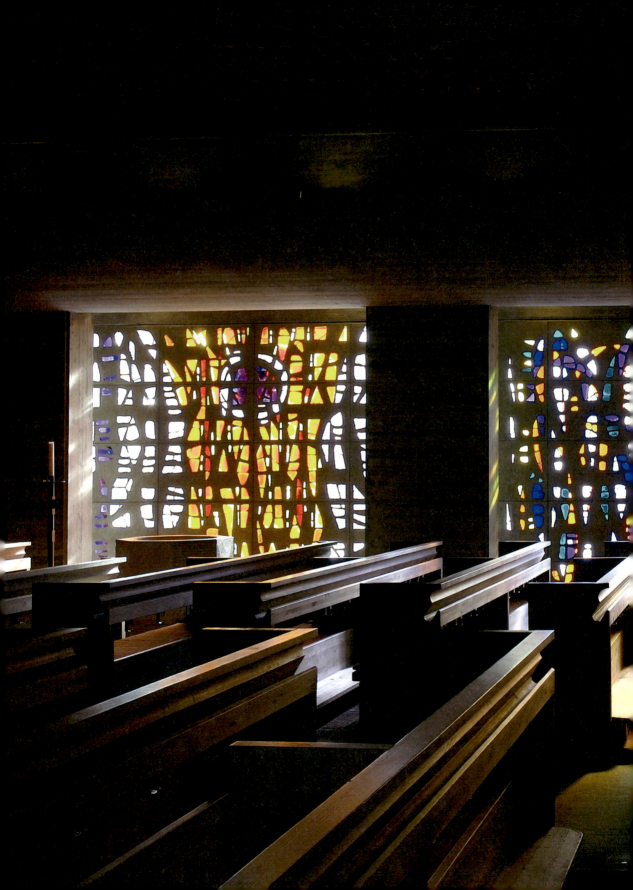

Finland
フィンランド

Chapel of the Resurrection
Erik Bryggman, 1941, Turku

2　3　4
5　6　7

復活礼拝堂 ｜エリック・ブリュッグマン｜ 1941 ｜トゥルク

北欧のロマンティシズムがこの上なく美しく表現されている礼拝堂。そのプロポーションと光の扱い方が秀逸だ。植物模様の扉から透ける白い正面壁に、向って右側（南側）の色ガラスを透過した光が射し込む。正面壁には、蔦が光の源へと向かう。正午の頃には、光が薄い角度で正面壁を照射する。壁面の質感や壁を伝う緑、柱に刻まれた彫りの浅いレリーフなどが一斉に浮かび上がる。天井高さの絶妙な操作によって作り出された明るい南側の領域からは、空間が森へと自然に流れ込む。

A chapel beautifully expressing the Nordic romanticism to the fullest degree. The proportion and handling of light are exquisite. Light through the colored glass on the right (south) side shines on the white front wall, visible through the plant-patterned door. Vines crawl on the front wall towards the light source. Shallow angled light illuminates the front wall around noon, casting light on the texture of the wall, plants on the wall, and a shallowly engraved relief on the pillar altogether. From the bright area on south, created by fine manipulation of the ceiling height, the space naturally flows into the forest.

1. 礼拝堂　祭壇方向（p092）
2. 礼拝堂　2階席より
3. 礼拝堂　南側の入口
4. 礼拝堂　南側の森へとつながる開口
5. 入口から祭壇方向
6. 会衆席に落ちる淡い光
7. 外観　正面
8. 断面図
9. 平面図

1. Chapel viewed facing the altar (p092)
2. Chapel viewed from a second floor seat
3. South entrance to the chapel
4. Opening connected to a forest on the south side of the chapel
5. View from the entrance, facing the altar
6. Light on the congregation seat
7. Exterior appearance of the front
8. Sectional plan
9. Floor plan

8　9

Mänistö Church
Juha Leiviskä, 1992, Kuopio

マンニスト教会 |ユハ・レイヴィスカ| 1992 |クオピオ

「光と音の建築家」と称される建築家レイヴィスカの白い空間には沈黙とドラマが潜む。白い面の重ね合わせによる垂直性が強調された空間。その配列は、光の動きを伴いながら、音楽のように美しい旋律を静的な空間に奏でる。アーティスト：マルック・パーッコネンとのコラボレーションで、柱の裏側にはアクリルペイントの淡い色彩のパネルが配置され、そこに反射して色付けられた光が、白い空間に淡い色彩のグラデーションをつけている。空間に浮遊する多数の照明器具も大きな魅力である。

Silence and drama are hidden in a white space designed by Leiviskä, known as the "architect of light and sound". The vertical feature of the space is enhanced by the accumulation of white surfaces. The arrangement plays a lovely melody in the static space, as if playing music, together with the movement of light. In collaboration with artist Markku Paakkonen, the acrylic painted, pale colored panels are arranged on the back of the pillars, and colored reflected light adds a pale colored gradation in the white space. The large number of light fixtures hung in the air is also very appealing.

1. 教会へのアプローチ
2. 協会　外観
3. 礼拝堂　入口より祭壇方向
4. 礼拝堂　祭壇の右手方向（p095）

1. Approach to the church
2. Exterior appearance of the church
3. Altar viewed from the church entrance
4. Right side of the altar in the church (p095)

5. サブ祭壇 (p095)
6. マルック・パーッコネンのカラーアート
   Markku paakkonen
7. 同
8. 照明器具
9. 断面図
10. 平面図

5. Sub-altar (p095)
6. Artwork of color by Markku Paakkonen
7. Same as above
8. Light fixture
9. Sectional plan
10. Floor plan

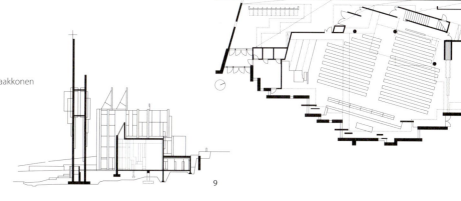

Vuoksenniska Church
Alvar Aalto, 1958, Imatra

ヴオクセンニスカ教会 |アルヴァル・アールト| 1958 |イマトラ

手の拳をモチーフにした有機的なフォルムは、音とともに光の効果が興味深い。内部には、さまざまな場所から質の異なる光が射し込む。正面右手から祭壇を照らす光、上部から祭壇を狙う光の砲、安定した明るさを与える左手のフラットな窓、外部と内部の異なる形態の隙間を埋める中空の採光部など。それらから直接射し込む光に、白いフォルムに反射する光が入り混じり、季節、時刻、天候によって多様な光の空間が作り出される。

The organic form with a motif of a fist has interesting effects of light, as well as sound. Light from various places with various qualities illuminate the interior: light from the front right that illuminates the altar; a spotlight from above aimed at the altar; the flat window on the left that provides a stable brightness; and the opening for daylight in midair that fills up the gap between the different forms of exterior and interior. Direct light from these sources is mingled with reflected light on the white form, resulting in the formation of diversified lighting conditions depending on the season, time, and weather.

1. 祭壇部から見上げる。光の砲は十字架を狙う
2. 外部と内部の隙間を埋める中空の採光部
3. エントランスの3つのトップライトからの光

1. Upward view from the altar. The spotlight is aimed at the crosses.
2. The opening for daylight in midair fills up the gap between the exterior and interior
3. Light from the three skylights in the entrance

4. 東側外観 (p098)
5. 外観に表現されたトップライト (p098)
6. 祭壇正面方向　夏至の早朝　スリット状の光 (p099)
7. 夏至の早朝　スリット状の光と3つの十字架の戯れ
8. 同
9. 同
10. 断面図
11. 平面図
12. 午後の西面からの光
13. 人工照明の点灯

4. Exterior appearance on the east side (p098)
5. Skylight expressed in the exterior appearance (p098)
6. Front view of the altar with a slit of light, in early morning on the summer solstice. (p099)
7. Early morning on the summer solstice. Interaction of the slit of light and three crosses.
8. Same as above
9. Same as above
10. Sectional plan
11. Floor plan
12. Afternoon light from the south
13. Illuminated artificial light

8

9

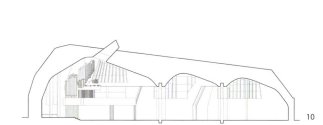
10

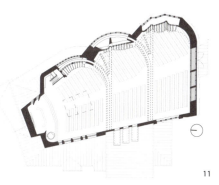
11

12

13

Nakkila Church
Erkki Huttunen, 1937, Nakkila

ナッキラ教会 ｜エルッキ・フットネン｜ 1937 ｜ナッキラ

フィンランドにおける初期機能主義建築の中で重要な例と位置付けられる教会。長い身廊に対して、祭壇方向に続くジグザグに折れ曲がった木製天井は、音響効果だけでなく興味深い視覚的効果も与える。正面には、右手の南を向くボックス状の採光装置から入射した光が、円弧状の正面壁と天井面の色彩を際立たせる。なおユハ・レイヴィスカ設計による白い木造の集会センターがこの教会に隣接して建つ。

A church characterized as a significant example among early functionalism architecture in Finland. A zigzag wooden ceiling, which leads to the altar along the long nave, gives a unique visual effect as well as an acoustic effect. In front, the light from the right side coming through the box-type natural lighting device facing the south, makes a great contrast of colors of circular-arc front wall and ceiling. A white wooden Congregation Center designed by Juha Leiviskä stands next to this church.

1. ナッキラ教会　内部祭壇方向 (p102)
2. 同　内部後方の天井と側窓
3. 同　祭壇南側の採光部外観
4. 同　正面外観
5. 同　内部照明点灯時
6. ナッキラ教会の集会センター（ユハ・レイヴィスカ設計、1970年）
7. 同　天井見上げ
8. ナッキラ教会　断面図
9. 同　平面図

1. Altar (p102)
2. Ceiling and side window at the back
3. Natural lighting device at the south of altar
4. Appearance
5. Inside with the lights on
6. Nakkila Congregation Center (designed by Juha Leiviskä, 1970)
7. Ceiling
8. Sectional Plan
9. Floor Plan

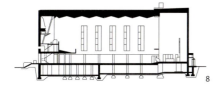
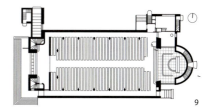

Otaniemi Chapel
Kaija & Heikki Siren, 1957, Espoo, near Helsinki

オタニエミ礼拝堂

| カイヤ&ヘイッキ・シレーン | 1957 | エスポー、ヘルシンキ近郊

アールト設計のヘルシンキ工科大学（現アールト大学）敷地内の森にひっそりと佇む礼拝堂。正面ガラスの外に置かれた十字架への連続性、決して対立しないフィンランドにおける建築と自然の関係性を象徴するシレーンの代表作。祭壇正面は北向きのため、南側背後から光が射し込む。傾斜屋根越しに光を受けた森の明るさが室内に入り、冬には雪の反射光がほんのりと天井を照らす。雪の白さや夏の緑に映える十字架は、この建築を世界に知らしめるに十分な象徴的なモニュメントだ。

The chapel quietly stands in a forest within the site of the Helsinki University of Technology (Aalto University), designed by Aalto. The chapel is a masterpiece of Siren, representing the never-conflicting relationship between architecture and nature in Finland via the continuation to the cross at the outside of the front glass wall. Light enters from the south side at the back of the north-facing altar. The brightness of the sunlit forest behind the inclined roof enters the room, and light reflected on snow dimly illuminates the ceiling in winter. The cross stands out against the whiteness of snow and the green of summer is a symbolic monument, which is enough to make the world aware of this architecture.

1. 祭壇背後のガラスごしの十字架　雪景色 (p104)
2. 夏の十字架
3. 天井木製架構の見上げ
4. 正面　外観
5. 平面図
6. 断面図

1. Snowy cross viewed through the glass wall behind the altar (p104)
2. Cross in summer
3. Wooden frame on the ceiling, viewed from below
4. Exterior appearance of the front
5. Floor plan
6. Sectional plan

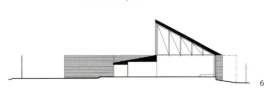

St. Henry's Ecumenical Art Chapel
Matti Sanaksenaho, 2005, Turku

聖ヘンリ・エキュメニカル礼拝堂 | マッティ・サナクセンアホ | 2005 | トゥルク

銅板により鈍い光を放つ特徴的なシルエットが地盤から屹立する。あえて長い距離をとるように設定された、緩やかなアプローチスロープを回り込む。方向転換して内部に入ると、一変して松の構造材がむき出しになった暖かみのある空間が祭壇方向へと細長く展開する。先端のアートガラスによって囲いとられた明るい領域が、祭壇方向を強調している。アートガラスの繊細なパターン、トップライトのディテールなども見所である。

1. 祭壇とアートガラス
2. 祭壇を囲むガラススリット
3. 入口より祭壇を見る
4. トップライト見上げ
5. トップライト外観
6. 外観
7. 平面図
8. 断面図
9. 礼拝堂 祭壇方向（p107）

1. Altar and art glass
2. Glass slit
3. Chapel viewed from the entrance
4. Skylight viewed from below
5. Skylight viewed from outside
6. Exterior appearance
7. Sectional plan
8. Floor plan
9. Full view of the chapel facing the altar(p107)

The characteristic silhouette with dull light reflected on copper panels towers above the ground. The gently sloped, folded approach was intentionally designed to elongate the length. Entering the interior after turning around, the scene changes and a narrow space with a warm atmosphere, having exposed structural members made of pine wood, develops towards the altar. The bright area at the end, framed with art glass, heightens the direction of the altar. The delicate pattern of the art glass and the detail of the skylight are also must-see items.

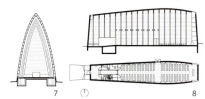

Viikki Church
JKMM Architects, 2005, Helsinki

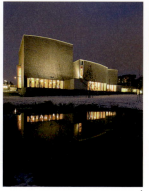

ヴィーッキ教会 ｜JKMM アーキテクツ｜2005｜ヘルシンキ

環境共生を目指す学園都市ヴィーッキにある教会。大小異なるホールの大きさがそのまま外観に表現され、ホール内部では、側面下方から入る光が床に反射し天井の木組みをあらわにする。天井高によって天井へ届く光量も異なり、空間の大きさの違いが光の拡散にも影響を与えている。大ホールの礼拝堂、祭壇正面の壁には、マホガニー合板に葡萄が描かれている。正午近く、壁画と平行に光が射し込む時、祭壇や十字架はシルエットとなり、銀箔面が浮かび上がる。

1. 祭壇 正午頃の光（p108）
2. 礼拝堂
3. 木製ルーバーの鐘楼
4. 水面に反映する柿葺きの外観
5. 天井を見上げる
6. 断面図

1. Altar in midday light (p108)
2. Church interior
3. Belfry with wooden louvers
4. Reflection in water of the exterior with shingled wall
5. Ceiling viewed from below
6. Sectional plan

A church in the academic city of Viikki, aiming to become environmentally friendly. The big and small sizes of the halls are directly reflected on the exterior appearance. In the interior of the halls, the wooden frame on the ceiling is revealed by light from the lower side walls reflected from the floor. The amount of light that reaches the ceiling differs depending on the ceiling height, and the size differences of the spaces also influence the light diffusion. Grapes are drawn on the mahogany plywood on the front wall behind the altar in the chapel of the large hall. Around noon, when light enters parallel to the wall painting, the altar and cross turn into silhouette, highlighting the silver foil on the surface.

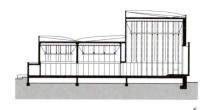

1

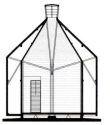

2

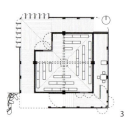

3

Kärsämäki Church
Lassila Hirvilammi Architects, Anssi Lassila, 2004, Kärsämäki

カルサマキ教会 | ラッシラ・ヒルヴィランミ・アーキテクツ、アンシ・ラッシラ | 2004 | カルサマキ

明るい平原と空を背景に黒いシルエットが浮かぶ。遠方からすでに光のシークエンスは始まっている。全体像をみせずに折れ曲がり、見え隠れしながら、鐘楼をくぐり、教会入口にアプローチする。外周には黒い外皮をもつ空間があり、可動ルーバーなどで調光が行われる。その内側、入れ子状に包まれた礼拝堂には唯一外界との接点として設けられたランタンからの光が射し込む。その光に加えて、外周の空間を介して侵入する横からの光が、礼拝堂内部の光の状態を変化させる。ログのテクスチャー、コールタールの塗られた壁面などに、伝統的なテクスチャーと光の効果を感じる。

1. 外観
2. 断面図
3. 平面図
4. 礼拝堂への入口
5. 礼拝堂祭壇方向
6. 礼拝堂 ランタンを見上げる
7. 礼拝堂 入口方向見返し
8. 礼拝堂 ランタンを見上げる

1. Exterior appearance
2. Sectional plan
3. Floor plan
4. Church entrance
5. Church hall viewed facing the altar
6. Lantern in the church, viewed from below
7. Church entrance from inside
8. Lantern viewed from below

A black silhouette stands against the background of a sunny plain and sky; the sequence of light already begins from far back. Approaching on a winding path with only part of the building visible, the church entrance is located after passing under the belfry with occasional view. A space with a black outer shell surrounds the outside of the building, and light in the space is adjusted with movable louvers. Inside of the space, the enclosed church hall is illuminated by light from a lantern, which is constructed as the only interface with the outside world. In addition, sideways light from the outside space enters and changes the lighting conditions within the church hall. The traditional texture and effect of light can be felt in such items as the texture of logs, and the coal tar painted walls.

Temppeliaukio Church
Timo & Tuomo Suomalainen, 1969, Helsinki

2　　　　　　　　　　　　　　　3　　　　　　　　　　　　　　　4

5

1. 礼拝堂（p112）
2. 銅板貼りの階上席のヴォリューム
3. 祭壇
4. 銅板の天井に反射する光
5. 集合住宅に囲まれた岩盤の敷地と円環状トップライト
6. 断面図
7. 平面図

1. Church interior (p112)
2. Volume of the balcony using copper panels
3. Altar
4. Light reflected on the copper panel ceiling
5. Rocky site surrounded by housing complexes and ring-shaped skylight
6. Sectional plan
7. Floor plan

6

テンペリアウキオ教会 ｜ティモ&トゥオモ・スオマライネン｜ 1969 ｜ヘルシンキ

「岩の教会」として親しまれているヘルシンキ中心部にある観光名所。集合住宅に囲われた円形の敷地の中心に、花崗岩の岩盤をくり抜いて作られている。洞窟に入る様に控えめな入口から入り、ひんやりとした岩肌を伝いながら礼拝堂にたどり着く。円形にくり抜かれた半地下の空間に、環状トップライトからの光が射し込み、円形の銅板天井には鈍い光が反射する。音響効果も良く、室内楽コンサートなどさまざまな催しにも利用されている。

Known as the "Church of the Rock", this church is a tourist attraction in central Helsinki. Granite rock was excavated to build the church at the center of the round site surrounded by housing complexes. Entering through the modest entrance, as if entering a cave, visitors reach the church space while feeling the coolness of the rock. In the semi-underground space, excavated into a round shape, light from the ring-shaped skylight enters, and the round-shaped copper panel ceiling dimly reflects the light. Due to the excellent acoustics, the church space is frequently used for various events, including chamber music concerts.

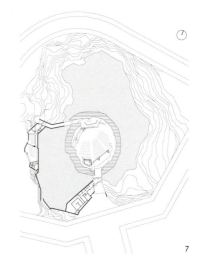

7

113

Kaleva Church
Raili & Reima Pietilä, 1966, Tampere

1. 礼拝堂　祭壇方向（p114）
2. 外観　見上げ
3. 丘にそびえ立つ外観
4. 天井を見上げる
5. 素材表面をなめるように侵入する光
6. 平面図
7. 断面図

1. Church viewed facing the altar (p114)
2. Exterior viewed from below
3. Exterior of the church, towering on a hill
4. Ceiling viewed from below
5. Light shines on the material surface as if crawling
6. Floor plan
7. Sectional plan

カレヴァ教会　｜ライリ&レイマ・ピエティラ｜ 1966 ｜タンペレ

幹線道路分岐点の小高い場所に建つ教会。ムーミン谷博物館が併設されていたタンペレ市立図書館（Tampere City Library/1986, Tampere）でも有名なピエティラ夫妻の代表作。設計当初の外装はコンクリート打放しだったが、タイルに変更されている。有機的なカーブを持ち、屹立する構造体の隙間から侵入する光。季節や時刻によって異なるスリットから直射光が侵入する。粗いテクスチャに金色の光が横切り、垂直性を強く感じる空間の中で光が刻々と動き回る。

Located on an elevated site near a junction of a major highway, the church is a masterpiece of the architect couple Raili and Reima Pietilä, who are famous for designing the Tampere City Library (1986, Tampere) with the Moominvalley Museum. The exterior was finished with tiles, changed from as-cast concrete in the original design. Light penetrates through gaps made on the organically curved, towering structure. Direct sunlight enters from different slits, depending on the season and time. Golden light crosses on the rough texture, and the light continues moving every second in the space with profound vertical features.

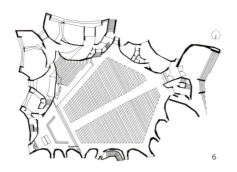

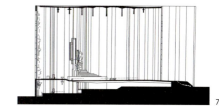

Malmi Church
Malmin kirkko, Kristian Gullichsen, 1980, Helsinki

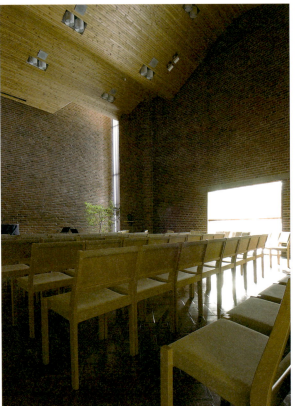

マルミ教会 | クリスティアン・グリクセン | 1980 | ヘルシンキ

暖かみのある素材と柔らかいフォルムが特徴で、礼拝堂正面における煉瓦壁は圧巻である。上部および側部のスリットからの光を受け、美しい光のグラデーションをみせる壁面に十字架が浮かび上がる。その右横の膨らみをもった空間では、上方から水盤を狙った光が落ち、祭壇方向からの光が床に刻まれる。サブホールのうねった木製の天井は、柔らかい光と音響効果を与えている。中庭などの外部も含め、教会全体が人間的で親密なスケール感覚に溢れている。

1. サブホール
2. 水盤と光
3. 水盤部のトップライト外部詳細
4. 平面図
5. 礼拝堂　正面壁を伝う光（p117）

1. Sub hall
2. Water stoup and light
3. Exterior detail of the skylight above the water stoup
4. Floor plan
5. Light on the front wall of the church (p117)

The church has a characteristic round form, using materials with warmth. The brick front wall of the church space is overwhelming. Illuminated by light through the slits above and on the sides, a beautiful gradation of light appears on the wall where the cross is highlighted. In the projected area on the right side, light from above falls onto the water stoup, and light from the altar direction is cast on the floor. The wavy wooden ceiling of the sub hall provides soft light and acoustic effects. The entire church, including the outside parts such as the courtyard, is filled with a humanly and intimate sense of scale.

Kamppi Chapel of Silence
K2S Architects, 2012, Helsinki

1. 礼拝堂 (p118)
2. 外観
3. 礼拝堂天井見上げ
4. 平面図
5. 断面図

1. Chapel (p118)
2. Exterior appearance
3. Chapel ceiling viewed from below
4. Floor plan
5. Sectional plan

静寂の礼拝堂 | K2S 建築設計事務所 | 2012 | ヘルシンキ

ヘルシンキの中心地カンピショッピングセンター前の広場に突如現れる礼拝堂。その形態と色彩は通り行く人の興味を引きつける。広場を訪れた人が自由に入り、静寂の時と空間を体験し、忙しい日常の中で心を安らかにする場として、ルーテル教会ヘルシンキ教区と市の福祉課が共同運営している。フィンランドらしい自然で自由な感覚の現れとも思える企画だ。卵型をした礼拝堂は積層された集成材の壁面にトップライトからの自然光が伝い落ちる。内部の人工照明は、外の光の状態に合わせてコンピューターで制御され、常に安定した光の環境が保たれる。

The chapel abruptly comes into sight in the square in front of the Kamppi Shopping Center in central Helsinki. The form and color attract the attention of passersby. The chapel is co-managed by the Helsinki Lutheran Church and the Social Services Department of the City of Helsinki, as a place where visitors to the square can freely enter, experience a silent moment and space, and calm themselves in the busy everyday life. This project seems like a representation of the spontaneous and free sense of Finland. In the egg-shaped chapel, natural light through the skylight falls on the wall of layered laminated lumber. The artificial lighting for the interior space is controlled by computer depending on the outdoor light conditions to maintain a stable light environment.

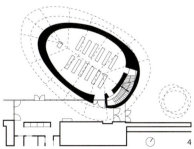
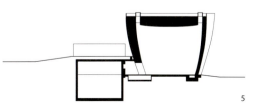

Harju Funeral Chapel Renovation and Extention
Juha Leiviskä, 1998, Mikkeli

1

ハルユ葬儀礼拝堂改修・増築工事 |ユハ・レイヴィスカ| 1998 |ミッケリ

マルッティ・ヴァリカンガス (Martti Välikangas) によって1936年に建てられた初期近代建築様式の礼拝堂に対する改修・増築工事。礼拝堂の主たる改修は、緩やかな円弧壁をもつ新しい祭壇の空間を付加し、そこに側面から光を取り込み白いリネンのタペストリーを輝かせるというものだが、最小限の操作でこれほど豊かな瞬間がつくれるのかと驚愕させられる。このタペストリーアートは、カイヤ・ポイユラ作 (Kaija Poijula)。かつての祭壇にあった青いカラーリングは、エーテルのように漂う、色付けられた青い反射光に代えられている。

1. 礼拝堂内部全景
2. 礼拝堂外観
3. 祭壇周り。光を受けるリネンのタペストリーと左手に浮かぶ青い反射光 (p121)

1. Full view of the chapel interior
2. Exterior appearance of the chapel designed by Martti Välikangas
3. Sunlit linen tapestry and blue reflection on the left near the altar (p121)

A renovation/extension project for an early-modern architecture style chapel by Martti Välikangas, built in 1936. The focus of the renovation was an addition of a new altar space with a gently curved wall, where the white linen tapestry dazzles by sideways light. It is astonishing to see that minimal changes could create such a moment of abundance. The tapestry is an artwork of Kaija Poijula. The blue color in the existing altar was replaced with blue-colored reflective light that lingers like ether.

2

4. 祭壇部上部見上げ
5. 光を受けたタペストリー　詳細
　カイヤ・ポイユラ作（Kaija poijula）
6. 断面図
7. 平面図
8. 光を受けたタペストリー見上げ (p123)

4. Above the altar, viewed from below
5. Detail of the sunlit tapestry by Kaija Poijula
6. Sectional plan
7. Floor plan
8. Sunlit linen tapestry viewed from below (p123)

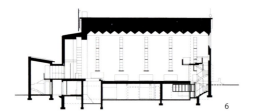
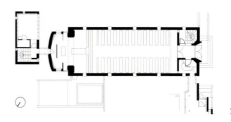

Kuokkala
Lassila Hirvilamm, Ar[...]

1. 礼拝堂　祭壇方向 (p124)
2. 礼拝堂　天井見上げ
3. 休憩スペース
4. 外観
5. 平面図
6. 断面図

1. Church hall viewed facing the altar (p124)
2. Church hall ceilling viewed from below
3. Rest area
4. Exterior appearance
5. Floor plan
6. Sectional plan

クオッカラ教会 | ラッシラ・ヒルヴィランミ・アーキテクト、アンシ・ラッシラ | 2008 | ユヴァスキュラ

カルサマキ教会 (p110) と同じ設計者による中部フィンランドの主要都市に建てられた3作目の教会建築は、外部と内部の形態の関係づけが興味深い。削り落とすように形作られたような独特な形態の外観に対し、礼拝堂内部では、菱形に組まれた木の格子によるもう一枚の表皮が柔らかく内部空間を形づくっている。頂部のスカイライトからの光が堂内を満たし、正面壁には木製の装飾が光を受けて浮かび上がる。ギャラリーを挟んで両側にある礼拝堂と教区ホールは、大きな祭礼の空間として一体的にも使える。

A church located in a major city in central Finland, the third church building by the architect who designed the Kärsämäki Church. It has an interesting association between the exterior and interior forms: the unique exterior seems as if formed by sculpturing, while the interior space of the church is softly formed by another layer of skin, consisting of diamond-patterned wooden lattices. Light through the skylight at the top fills the interior space, and the sunlit wooden decoration on the front wall stands out. The church hall and the parish meeting hall, located on both sides of the gallery, can be used together as a space for larger festivals.

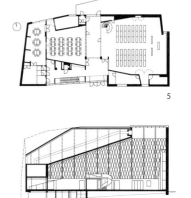

Chapel of St. Lawrence
Avanto Architects, 2011, Vantaa, near Helsinki

1

聖ローレンス礼拝堂

|アヴァント・アーキテクツ| 2011 |ヴァンター、ヘルシンキ近郊|

墓地内に建つ礼拝堂。大きさの異なる3つの礼拝堂が直行する壁によって一つにまとめられて全体を構成する。それぞれの礼拝堂へは外部から壁面沿いに庭を通りながらアプローチするが、煉瓦積みの白い壁面に沿って連続するトップライトからの光によって、低く薄暗い空間から天井の高い明るい空間へと導かれる。礼拝堂で使用している素材は、漆喰仕上げの煉瓦、自然石、緑青を吹いた銅板と金網など、敷地周辺で使われているものと類似のものだ。光を受けるアクリルのアートワークも興味深い。

A chapel located in a cemetery. Three various-sized chapels are nested within an orthogonal wall to form the entire building. Each chapel is accessible from outside via a garden along a wall. With light through the continuous skylight along the white brick wall, visitors are lead from a dimly lit, low-ceiling space to a bright, high-ceiling space. Materials used for the chapels are similar to what is used in the neighborhood area, including plaster finished bricks, fieldstones, patinated copper panels, and metal meshes. The illuminated acrylic art work is also interesting.

1. 大礼拝堂
2. 大礼拝堂へのアプローチ
3. 連続する3つの入口
4. アクリルワーク
5. 小礼拝堂
6. 平面図
7. 断面図

1. Large chapel
2. Approach to the large chapel
3. Three entrances next to each other
4. Acrylic art work
5. Small chapel
6. Floor plan
7. Sectional plan

Vatiala Funerary Chapel
Viljo Revell, 1960, Kangasala, near Tampere

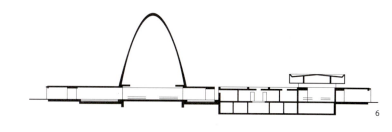

ヴァティアラ礼拝堂 ｜ヴィルヨ・レヴェル｜ 1960 ｜カンガサラ、タンペレ近郊

周囲の松林の垂直性に対して水平なコンクリート屋根が続く中、放物線を描く大礼拝堂の屋根と小礼拝堂の吊られた屋根が突出するこの建築は、構造家パーヴォ・シムラ（Paavo Simula）とのコラボレーションである。池に挟まれた大礼拝堂では、池に反射した光がカーブを描く天井面に映り込み、揺らぎながら刻々とその軌跡を刻んでいく。小礼拝堂では、天井と壁の接合部から入り込む光が、構造的に浮いた天井を劇的に強調している。

1. 大礼拝堂 天井面を照らす池の反射光（p128）
2. 礼拝堂外観
3. 大礼拝堂横のプール
4. 待合室に落ちるトップライトの光
5. 小礼拝堂
6. 断面図

The parabola-shaped roof of the large chapel and the suspended roof of the small chapel stand out among the concrete roofs that spread horizontally against the vertical features of the surrounding pine forest. This architecture was built under collaboration with structural engineer Paavo Simula. In the large chapel between ponds, light reflected from the ponds shimmers on the curved ceiling, and moves along its trajectory over time. In the small chapel, light enters from the joints between the ceiling and the walls, dramatically enhancing the structurally suspended ceiling.

1. Light reflected from the ponds illuminates the ceiling of the large chapel (p128)
2. Exterior appearance of the chapel
3. Pool beside the large chapel
4. Light from the skylight falling on the waiting room
5. Small chapel
6. Sectional plan

Pirkkala Church
Käpy & Simo Paavilainen, 1994, Pirkkala, near Tampere

1

2

3

4

6

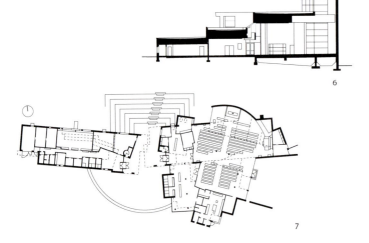
5

8

ピルッカラ教会 |キャプ ＆シモ・パーヴィライネン| 1994 |ピルッカラ、タンペレ近郊

礼拝施設と幼児保育施設を主とした複合体。建物へのアプローチの先には、二つの棟と屋根の重なりに囲い取られた草原と森と空が広がる。礼拝堂の緩やかな円弧状の白い正面壁には、透明ガラスの天窓と側窓からの直射日光によって光の軌跡が描かれる。礼拝堂の中間部で天井に貫入する立体的なスカイライト、低い天井部で外へとつながる窓、エントランスの大きなガラス面など、複雑な構成をとりながら、各所の開口部から入射する光によって、明るさの確保と立体的な光の分布が実現している。

1. 外観　アプローチ
2. 二つの棟と屋根に囲い取られた景色
3. 外観　スカイライトの連なり
4. 立体的なスカイライトとその先の外へとつながる窓
5. 礼拝堂　入口を振り返る
6. 断面図
7. 平面図
8. 礼拝堂　祭壇と正面壁

A complex building mainly consisting of a church and childcare facility. Grassland, forest, and sky, framed by two overlapping buildings and roofs, spread out beyond the approach. Direct sunlight through the skylight and side windows with transparent glass leaves traces of light on the gently curved, white front wall of the church. Although having a complicated composition (e.g., a three-dimensional skylight that penetrates into the ceiling at the central part of the church, a window in the low-ceiling area that is connected to the outside, and a large glass surface at the entrance), brightness is ensured and three-dimensional light distribution is realized by light entering from openings at various locations.

1. Exterior appearance and approach to the church
2. View framed by the two buildings and roofs
3. Exterior appearance with a series of skylights
4. Three-dimentional skylight and window that leads to the exterior behind it
5. Church entrance viewed from inside
6. Sectional plan
7. Floor plan
8. Altar and front wall of the church

Norway
ノルウェー

St. Hallvard's Church and Monastery
Lund and Slaatto, 1966, Oslo

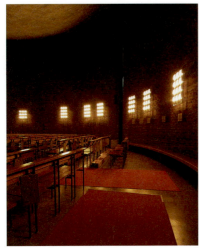

聖ハルヴェード教会および修道院 |ルンド＆スラット| 1966 |オスロ

傾斜地にマッシブな外観を呈する赤い煉瓦と灰色のコンクリートを主材料としたカトリックの教会と修道院。円形の礼拝堂とその周囲の諸室の平面構成は、図と地の明解な関係性を示している。その関係性は、屋根と壁の断面形においても見出せる。頭上には、コンクリートの重々しい天井が覆いかぶさり、壁と天井の隙間から自然光が礼拝堂に導かれるが、その光量はかなり少なく、堂内は深い闇が支配し神秘性を醸し出す。闇に目が慣れてくると、その中に立体的に構成される階段室などがうっすらと浮かび上がってくる。

A Catholic church and monastery with a massive exterior appearance on a sloped site, which mainly consist of red bricks and gray concrete. The plan composition with the round church and surrounding rooms indicates a clear relationship between the figure and the ground. The relationship can also be found in the cross sectional shape of the roof and walls. The massive concrete ceiling covers overhead. Although natural light enters into the church through gaps between the walls and ceiling, the light is weak and the interior is dominated by deep darkness, creating a mysterious atmosphere. Once eyes are adjusted, three-dimensional objects, such as a stair hall, can be faintly recognized.

1. 礼拝堂　祭壇方向 (p134)
2. 礼拝堂　側方
3. 礼拝堂　階段方向
4. 外観
5. 断面図
6. 平面図

1. Church interior viewed facing the altar (p134)
2. Side of the church interior
3. Church interior viewed facing the stairs
4. Exterior appearance
5. Sectional plan
6. Floor plan

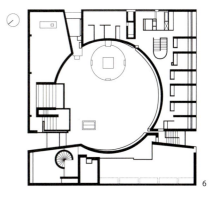

Mortensrud Church
Jensen & Skodvin Arkitektkontor, 2002, Oslo

モルテンスルッド教会 | イェンセン&スコドヴィン設計事務所 | 2002 | オスロ

オスロ市内の松の木の生える小さな丘の上に建つ教会。切妻屋根を持つ細長い礼拝堂の床には、敷地に当初より存在した岩が露出する。教会の外壁の内側には、入れ子状に鉄骨の構造材の間を石で埋めた内壁が立つ。西側面と祭壇方向正面は、壁の下部は開放されているが、上部は石壁からの砕かれた光が礼拝堂を包み込む。鉄骨の構造材や天井の金属折板はそのまま表現され、全体的に工業的な軽さと明るさに満ちた教会だ。

This gabled roof church is located on a small hill with pine tree vegetation in the city of Oslo. There is a rock on the long, narrow church floor, which was on the original site and left exposed. Inside the exterior wall of the church, interior walls consisting of a steel framework filled with stones are erected. On the west side and front altar side, the bottoms of the walls are open, but fragmented light through the upper part of the stone walls enclose the church. The steel framework and folded metal plates on the ceiling are exposed, and the overall church is filled with an industrial lightness and brightness.

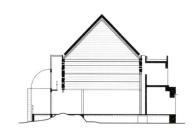

5. 断面図　Sectional plan

6. 平面図　Floor plan

1. 外観　見上げ
2. 礼拝堂　祭壇
3. 礼拝堂　石の内壁
4. 礼拝堂　祭壇方向全景　露出した岩 (p137)

1. Exterior appearance from below
2. Internal stone wall of the church
3. Altar in the church
4. Full view of the church facing the altar and the exposed rock (p137)

Bøler Church
Hansen-Bjørndal Arkitekter, 2004, Oslo

ボゥーラー教会 |ハンセン/ビョルンダール設計事務所| 2004 |オスロ

オスロ市内の幹線道路より少し昇った間口の広い細長敷地に建つ教会。中庭をうまく構成しながら造られた、幼稚園なども併設する大規模な複合体だ。石、コンクリート、鉄などの素材を用い幾何学的に構成されたストイックでシンプルな外観。一方、礼拝堂内部は、シンプルなヴォリューム構成であるが、明るい木材を主たる仕上げとし、ルーバーの使用や隅部に丸みをつけることなどにより柔らかさと清潔感を与える空間。正面壁には、自然光によって輝くステンドグラスが、低い位置で水平に帯状に廻る。

1. 正面外観
2. 大礼拝堂の前庭
3. 小礼拝堂横の中庭
4. 平面図
5. 大礼拝堂全景
6. 前室より大礼拝堂
7. 大礼拝堂内の副祭壇

---

1. Exterior appearance of the front
2. Front yard of the church
3. Courtyard on the side of the small hall
4. Floor plan
5. Full view of the church
6. Church viewed from the front room
7. Sub altar of the large church

The church is located at a narrow site with a wide frontage, a little bit elevated from a major highway in Oslo. This church is in a large-scale complex that includes facilities such as a kindergarten, and was built by skillfully utilizing a courtyard. The stoic and simple exterior appearance is geometrically composed with materials including stones, concrete, and iron. Meanwhile, the interior of the church has a simple volume composition. However, the space gives a sense of softness and cleanliness, due to the finish of mainly light-colored wood, use of louvers, and rounded corners. A horizontal strip of stained glass, illuminated by natural light, runs along the lower part of the front wall.

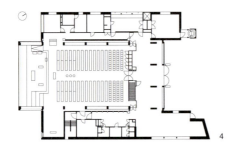

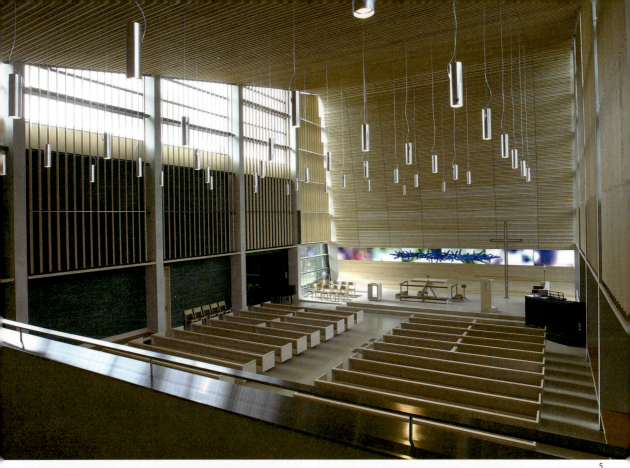

5

6
7

Vardåsen Church
Terje Grønmo, 2003, Asker, near Oslo

ヴァードオーセン教会 |テァイェ・グロンモ| 2003 |アスカー、オスロ近郊

森を背後に控えた草原の際に建つ教会。礼拝堂と幼児保育施設はエントランスホールを挟んで平行に配置されるが、礼拝中、礼拝堂の二階バルコニーからは透明ガラスを通して保育施設の様子がうかがえる。コンクリート打ち放しを基調とした礼拝堂は、下部の帯状に連続する外へとつながる窓からの光とトップライトから壁沿いを伝い降りる光の組み合わせからなるが、残念ながら訪れた際トップライトは塞がれていたために空間の魅力は大きく減じており、改めて光の分布の重要性を認識させられた。

1. 外観
2. 縦長スリット部　見上げ
3. 礼拝堂見下ろし
4. 断面図
5. 礼拝堂　祭壇後ろより見返り (p141)

1. Exterior appearance
2. Part with a tall slit viewed from below
3. Church viewed from above
4. Sectional plan
5. Church viewed from behind the altar (p141)

The church stands at the edge of a grassland in front of a forest. The church and childcare facility are located on each side of the entrance hall, arranged in parallel, so that the childcare facility behind transparent glass can be seen from the second floor balcony of the church during services. The church is basically made of as-cast concrete, and consists of a combination of lighting: light from the low ribbon windows that continue to the outside, and light that falls along the wall from the skylight. Unfortunately, the skylight was blocked when I visited, and the appeal of the space was significantly reduced. This made me recognize anew the importance of light distribution.

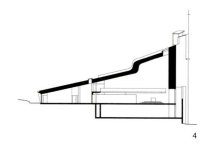

Tautra Mariakloster
Jensen & Skodvin Arkitektkontor, 2006, Tautra

2

3

4

タウトラ・マリア修道院 |イェンセン&スコドヴィン設計事務所| 2006 |タウトラ

トロンハイムフィヨルドの孤島に建つシトー会修道院。そこでは毎日、7回のお祈りと労働を基本とする修道女達の生活が静かに営まれている。海辺において厳しい自然環境から守るかのように、長方形の閉じた領域を切り取り、そこに礼拝の場と労働の場などが、7つの庭とととともに構成されている。礼拝堂では、フィヨルドに面する祭壇背後が透明ガラスになっており、外に広がる水面や樹木の揺らぎや音などを感じながら、そして木を格子状に組んだガラス屋根から降り注ぐ光と影や空の変化の中で、祈りと神との対話が繰り返される。

A Cistercian abbey on an isolated island in Trondheimsfjord, where a quiet life for nuns progresses, basically with seven daily prayer times and work. As if providing protection from the harsh natural environment along the seashore, a closed rectangular area is cut to compose places for prayer and work, along with seven gardens. In the church, a transparent glass wall is made behind the altar, facing a fjord. Prayers and conversations with God are repeated in the midst of the changing sky, the shade and light showering from the glass roof with a wooden latticework, and while feeling fluctuations and sounds of water and trees outside.

1. 修道院遠望 (p142-143)
2. 礼拝堂 夜明け前に瞑想する修道女
3. 夜明け頃の最初の祈りの時間帯 礼拝堂外観
4. 午後の礼拝
5. 礼拝堂 夏の夜明け (p145)

1. Distant view of the abbey (p142-143)
2. Meditating nun in the church before dawn
3. Exterior appearance of the church at the first prayer time around dawn
4. Afternoon prayer
5. Church in dawn in summer (p145)

6. 礼拝堂　正午ごろ　前室より礼拝堂
7. 礼拝堂　妻面および天井見上げ
8. 礼拝堂側面の中庭方向
9. 平面図
10. 断面図
11. 礼拝堂　午後遅くの光（p147）

6. Church viewed from the front room around noon
7. Church gable end and ceiling viewed from below
8. Side view of the church, facing the courtyard direction
9. Floor plan
10. Sectional plan
11. Church in mid afternoon light (p147)

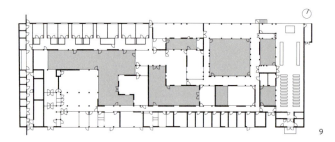
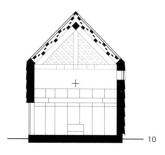

12. 屋根上より修道院全体を望む 奥に礼拝堂
13. フィヨルドを望める食事室
14. 談話室
15. 礼拝堂 海辺側 ガラスに映る夕日と水面
    外壁は、風合いの異なる石パネル張り (p149)

12. Panoramic view of the abbey from the rooftop. The church is at the back.
13. Refectory room with fjord view
14. Chapter room
15. Church facing the seashore. Evening sun and water are reflected on the glass surface. The exterior wall is variously textured stone panels (p149)

Sunrise glow on water behind the abbey
修道院裏フィヨルドの朝焼け

Brumunddal Church
Molle and Per Cappelen, 1965, Brumunddal

1. 外観
2. 礼拝堂　側部のスリット窓
3. 柿葺き屋根の詳細
4. 平面図
5. 礼拝堂　祭壇方向（p153）

ブルムンダール教会　|モレ&ペア・カペレン|　1965　|ブルムンダール

柿(こけら)葺き屋根による三角形のヴォリュームを持つ教会が、墓地を併設する森の木立の中でひっそりと建つ。その姿は何世紀も前から時を経て、そこにあったような佇まいだ。教会内部は、松の構造材・仕上げ材によって外観の形がそのまま表現される。祭壇背後の壁面は、材の向きを変えながら三重に構成された木製のルーバーと四角形に埋め込まれた青いステンドグラスが美しい光の調和を生み出している。両側面には水平に細長い窓が設けられ、礼拝堂全体の明るさを確保している。

1. Exterior appearance
2. Slit window on the side of the church
3. Detail of the shingled roof
4. Floor plan
5. Church viewed facing the altar (p153)

The shingled roof church with a triangular volume quietly stands on a woody site connected to a cemetery. It appears as if it were there for centuries. The exterior form of the church itself is expressed inside by a pine framework and finishing materials. On the wall behind the altar, a beautiful harmony of light is formed by the triple-layered louvers made of differently angled wood, and embedded square-shaped blue stained glass. Horizontally long slit windows on both sides ensure the overall brightness in the church.

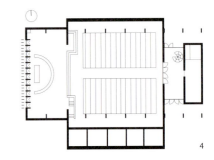

St. Magnus Church
Lund and Slaatto, 1988, Lillestrøm

聖マウヌス教会 |ルンド&スラット| 1988 |リレストルム

リズミカルに大きさを変えながら構成された主空間と従空間の組み合わせとそのヴォールト屋根の形態は、ルイス・カーンの名作キンベル美術館を思い起こさせるが、内部空間における光の扱いは大きく異なる。キンベル美術館では、直射日光を排除するために、反射板で天井面を照らしたのに対し、ここでは直射光がスリット状の光として射し込み、礼拝堂内を動き回る。静かな住宅地の中、周辺環境にも人間的で上品なスケール感を与え奉仕している。

Combination of a main space and auxjliary spaces with rhythmic variations in size, and the form of the vaulted roof inevitably reminds us of the Kimbell Art Museum by Louis Kahn; however, handling of light in the interior space is significantly different. In the Kimbell Art Museum, the ceilings were lit by reflectors to exclude direct sunlight, but in this church, slit-shaped direct sunlight enters the church space and moves around. The church also serves the surrounding environment in a quiet residential area by providing a humanly and elegant sense of scale.

1. 礼拝堂　主祭壇方向 (p154)
2. 外観
3. 礼拝堂全景　祭壇方向
4. 礼拝堂　パイプオルガン部
5. 断面図
6. 平面図

1. Church viewed facing the main altar (p154)
2. Exterior appearance
3. Full view of the church facing the altar
4. Pipe organ in the church
5. Sectional plan
6. Floor plan

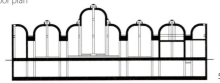

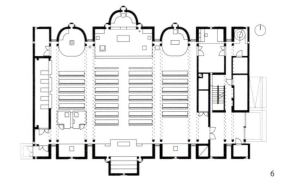

Knarvik Church
Reiulf Ramstad Architects, 2015, Isdalstø, near Bergen

クナーヴィク教会 │ レイウルフ・ラムスタッド設計事務所 │ 2015 │ イスダルスト、ベルゲン近郊

ベルゲン近くのフィヨルドに面し、岩場が露出する斜面地に建つ教会。平面図からはまったく想像ができないほどの大胆な外形は、白鳥の姿をモチーフにしたともいわれる。険しい環境の中でも際立つ鋭角的な外観は、フィヨルドを巡る観光船上からの遠距離でも認識出来るほどだ。外装は、エイジングを狙った無塗装の松材が用いられ燻し銀のように輝く。鋭角的な形態は内部空間においても表現され、天井にはオーロラライトと呼ばれる蛍光灯がその舞い降りる姿を表現している。北の地ならではのモチーフだ。

Facing a fjord near Bergen, the church stands on a sloped site with exposed rocks. The dynamic exterior form, completely beyond imagination by the floor plan alone, is said to have a motif of a swan. The acute angled building exterior stands out in the harsh environment, and is recognizable even from far-away sightseeing ships in the fjord. The exterior is finished with unpainted pine wood, aiming for an aging effect, and shines as if it were oxidized silver. The acute angled form is also expressed in the interior space. Fluorescent lights on the ceiling, called aurora lights, express the appearance of flying down: a motif unique to the northland.

1. 外観 (p156)
2. 礼拝堂 見上げ
3. 礼拝堂 祭壇方向
4. 教会主玄関
5. 断面図
6. 平面図

1. Exterior appearance (p156)
2. Church interior viewed from below
3. Church interior viewed facing the altar
4. Main entrance of the church building
5. Sectional plan
6. Floor plan

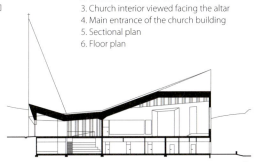
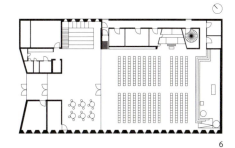

Arctic Cathedral
Jan Inge Hovig, 1965, Tromsø

1. 夕刻の外観
2. 屋根部詳細
3. 平面図
4. 礼拝堂 祭壇方向 (p159)
5. 対岸からの夜景 (p160-161)

1. Exterior appearance in evening
2. Detail of the roof
3. Floor plan
3. Church viewed facing the altar (p159)
4. Night view from the opposite shore (p160-161)

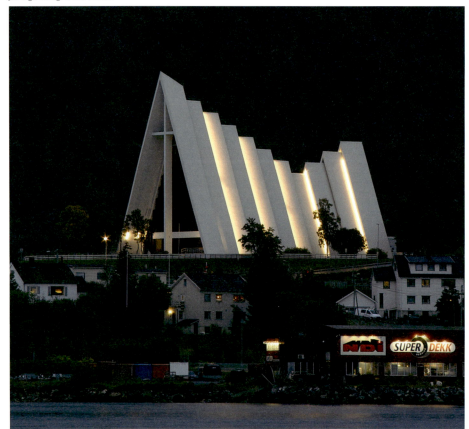

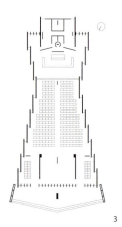

北極教会 | ヤン・インゲ・ホービ | 1965 | トロムソ

北緯約70度の北極圏の街トロムソ。最北の大学都市として、またオーロラや白夜体験地としても有名だ。その中心市街地より2キロの橋を渡った対岸にある教会。幅約3.5mのコンクリートパネルによる三角形状の屋根が高さを変え、ずれながら構成されている。その屋根の隙間は、内部に自然光を導き、夜間は内部の灯りを放出し、その構成を美しく際立たせる。青を基調とした美しいステンドグラスは、キリスト復活を描いたヨーロッパ最大級のものとのこと。街の重要なランドマークとして、閉堂後も夜中まで光を放ち、対岸からの夜景を楽しませてくれる。

The city of Tromsø in the Arctic Circle is located at about 70°N, and is famous as the northernmost academic city, as well as a place to experience the Aurora Borealis and white nights. The cathedral is on the opposite shore across a bridge, 2km from the city center. The building consists of misaligned triangular roofs of various heights, which are made of precast concrete and are about 3.5m wide. Gaps between the roofs allow natural light to enter the building in the daytime, while emitting light from the interior in the nighttime, enhancing the magnificence of the composition. Beautiful blue-toned stained glass, expressing the Resurrection of Christ, is the largest in Europe. As an important landmark, the cathedral emits light after open hours until late at night, providing an enjoyable night view from the opposite shore.

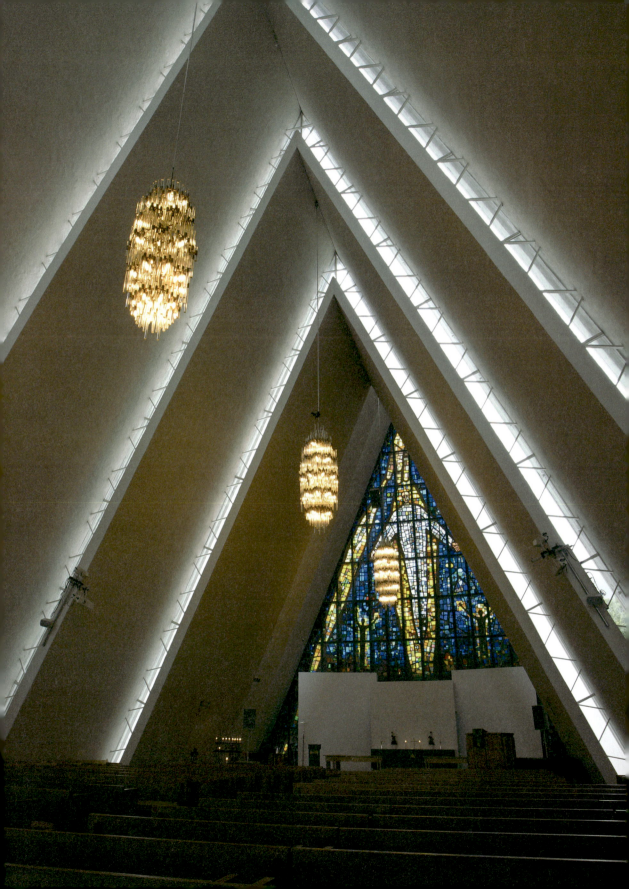

Iceland
アイスランド

Blue Lagoon in Grindavik
ブルーラグーン／グリンダヴィーク

Neskirkja Church
Áugust Pálsson, 1957, Reykjavik

2

3

ネス教会 | アウグスト・パルソン | 1957 | レイキャヴィーク

アイスランドの首都レイキャヴィークにおいて、近代的な方法で建設され最初に完成した教会で、大きさでは二番目を誇る。礼拝堂内部は、前方祭壇部より後方にかけて、天井がだんだんと高さを下げてくるが、それにあわせて側壁上部に設けられたスリット窓から祭壇方向へと自然光が導かれる。外観には天井高さの変化とスリット窓の構成が表現される。祭壇部右手には足下から天井までの幅の広い側窓があるが、青を基調としたステンドグラスの光が美しく印象的だ。

1. 礼拝堂　後方 (p166)
2. 外観
3. ホワイエのステンドグラス
4. 礼拝堂　十字架とステンドグラス (p168-169)

1. Rear of the church (p166)
2. Exterior appearance
3. Stained glass in Foyer
4. Cross and stained glass in the church (p168-169)

The first church built in a modern method in Reykjavik, the capital of Iceland, and the second largest in size. The ceiling height in the church space gradually lowers from the front altar to the rear. Natural light is accordingly directed towards the altar through the slit windows on the upper part of the side walls. The ceiling height transition and composition of the slit windows are expressed on the exterior. On the right side of the altar, a fat side window stretches from floor to ceiling, and light through the blue-toned stained glass is impressively beautiful.

Hallgrimskirkja Church
Guðjón Samúelsson, 1940-74, Reykjavik

2

ハルグリム教会 |グドジョン・サムエルソン| 1940 – 74 |レイキャヴィーク

市内を遠望出来る高台に建てられたレイキャヴィークで最も大きな教会。教会名はアイルランドの１７世紀の宣教師で詩人でもあったハルグリム・ペーターソン（1614-1674）にちなんで付けられた。73 メートルの高さはアイスランドの建物で６番目で、最上階は展望台としても機能している。その最高部まで左右からせり上がるダイナミックな外部形態は、表現主義建築とされることが多い。一方、外観とは対照的に内部は至ってシンプルな表現だ。この教会の建設には３４年もの年月を要している。

The largest church in Reykjavik, built on a hill with a view of the city. The church was named after Hallgrímur Pétursson (1614-1674), who was a 17th century missionary and poet in Iceland. The 73m church is the sixth highest building in Iceland, and the top floor serves as an observation deck. The dynamic exterior form, rising from both sides to the very tip, is often categorized as Expressionist architecture. In contrast to the exterior, the interior is quite simply expressed. Construction of this church took 34 years.

1. 正面外観（p170）
2. 礼拝堂
3. 外観　後方より（P172-173）

1. Exterior appearance of the front (p170)
2. Church interior
3. Exterior appearance from the back (p172-173)

Appendix

解説・資料編

北欧諸国の気候風土

北欧諸国の地勢と気候

　今回対象にしている北欧5カ国は、北極線66度以北の北極圏をも含む、緯度にしておよそ50度から70度の範囲に広がるが、メキシコ湾流から延長してヨーロッパ西岸に向かって流れる暖流「北大西洋海流」の影響で、高緯度の割には比較的温暖な気候である。ここでは各国の地勢と気候について概説したい。表左欄に、国ごとに、国土面積、森林率、水面積率などを、右欄には各国の首都および主要都市における季節ごとの平均気温、平均湿度、可照時間などをまとめたので、適宜参照されたい。

　デンマークはヨーロッパ大陸と陸続きのユトランド半島と首都コペンハーゲンのあるシェラン島、フェン島を中心に、大小約500の島々からなる。国土は日本の一割強で、九州より少し大きい程度である。森林は少なく（森林率11.8%）、国土はおおむね平坦であり（最高高さ173メートル）、都市部を離れると小麦を中心とした畑が緩やかに連なる牧歌的な風景が広がり、酪農も盛んである。気候については、5カ国の中でも緯度が低いため最も温暖である。降水量は少なく、他の4カ国と異なり、雪が降り積もることは少ない。

　スウェーデンは、日本の約1.2倍の面積、日本全土に北海道をもう一つ足した程度の大きさで、北欧諸国の中では一番の大国である。スカンジナビア半島の中央、東側に位置し、西側は、標高2,000m程度のなだらかなスカンジナビア山脈が南北に連なっており（最高高さ2104メートル）、ノルウェーに面する。一方、東側はボスニア湾を挟んでフィンランドがあるが、北部においては陸上で繋がる。なお、およそ北極線以北のフィンランド、スウェーデン、ノルウェー、そしてロシアにまたがる北の地域は、ラップランド地方と呼ばれ、この地域の先住民族であるサーミ人が伝統的に住んでいる。

　スウェーデンの国土には、森林が多く（森林率66.9%）、湖沼も多い（水面積率8.7%）。平野部はあるがそれほど広大ではない。肥沃な土地は南部のスコーネ県しかなく、中部から北部は農業には適さず酪農が主である。

　フィンランドは、北側はノルウェー、西側はスウェーデンと国境を接し、西はボスニア湾、南西はバルト海、南はフィンランド湾に面する。東から南東にかけてはロシアと陸上で国境を接する。面積は日本の約9割で、国土の大半は平坦な地形であるが、北および北東部には一部高地がある（最高高さ1324メートル）。森と湖は北欧5カ国の中で最も多く（森林率73.9%、水面積率9.4%）、「森と湖の国」と呼ばれることが多い。

　気候に関しては、スウェーデンとフィンランドは、同緯度に属しながらも、北大西洋海流の影響を直接受けるノルウェーやアイスランドに比べて、冬は厳しい寒さになり、北部では平均気温が氷点下10度以下となる地域も多い。また冬期には港や湖なども凍ることが多い。

　ノルウェーは、スカンジナビア半島の西岸に位置し、国土面積は日本の9割弱の大きさである。北極海およびノルウェー海に面し、海岸には氷河による浸食作用によって形成された複雑な地形の湾・入り江「フィヨルド」が発達している。陸地の殆どをスカンジナビア山脈が占めるため、平地はほとんどない（最高高さ2469m）。

　北大西洋海流の分枝であるノルウェー海流の影響を強く受け、山間部を除くとスウェーデンやフィンランドよ

国	国土				気候						首都
	国土面積 (㎡)	最高高さ (m)	森林率 (%)	水面積率 (%)	平均気温 (℃)	平均相対湿度 (%)	降水量 (mm)	可照時間/日 (h)*	南中時太陽高度 (°)*	季節	
アイスランド	103,000	2,110	0.50%	2.70%	0.6	77.4	82.5	12.5	26	3月/春分*	レイキャヴィーク (北緯64.8度)
					9.5	79	43.4	21.3	49	6月/夏至*	
					8	79	75	12.2	26	9月/秋分*	
					0.6	78.5	97	4.3	3	12月/冬至*	
ノルウェー	323,787	2,469	30.70%	6.00%	-5.2	80	61.7	12.3	31	3月/春分*	オスロ (北緯59.5度)
					13.9	66	75.4	18.8	54	6月/夏至*	
					10	79	82.2	12.2	30	9月/秋分*	
					-4.6	89	62,2	6.0	7	12月/冬至*	
フィンランド	338,431	1,324	73.90%	9.40%	-1.9	80	54.4	12.3	30	3月/春分*	ヘルシンキ (北緯60.1度)
					14.6	66	59.3	19.0	53	6月/夏至*	
					10.7	85	65.3	12.5	30	9月/秋分*	
					-3.1	93	56.9	6.8	7	12月/冬至*	
スウェーデン	450,295	2,104	66.90%	8.70%	6.6	74	37.2	12.3	31	3月/春分*	ストックホルム (北緯59.2度)
					14.7	65	52.3	18.7	54	6月/夏至*	
					11.3	78	64.7	9.7	30	9月/秋分*	
					-0.8	88	44.4	8.0	7	12月/冬至*	
デンマーク	43,094	171	11.80%	1.60%	3.4	82	41.8	12.3	35	3月/春分*	コペンハーゲン (北緯55.4度)
					15.6	72	60	17.5	58	6月/夏至*	
					14	78	58.8	12.2	34	9月/秋分*	
					2.5	85	48.6	7.0	11	12月/冬至*	
日本	377,972	3,776	68.20%	0.80%	9.4	55	117.5	12.2	55	3月/春分*	東京 (北緯38度)
					22.1	72	167.7	14.7	78	6月/夏至*	
					23.8	71	209.9	12.2	54	9月/秋分*	
					8.7	52	51	9.8	31	12月/冬至*	

1) 国土面積：https://ja.wikipedia.org/wiki/国の面積順リスト
2) 最高高さ：https://ja.wikipedia.org/wiki/国別の最高地点一覧
3) 森林率：世界各国の森林率 資料：FAO「The Global Forest Resources Assessment 2005」
4) 水面積：各国のwikipediaより
5) 平均気温：国立天文台編『平成25年 理科年表』(丸善、2013)より、1981-2010年の平年値。但し、ストックホルム1982-1994年の平年値
6) 相対湿度：同、1961-1990年の平年値。但し、ストックホルムとヘルシンキは1982-1967年の平年値。東京は1981-2010年の平年値
   但し、コペンハーゲンは、DANISH METEOROGICAL INSTITUTE MINISTRY OF TRASPORT TECHNICAL REPORT 99-5, COPENHAGEN 1999より1961-1990年の平年値
7) 降水量：同『平成25年 理科年表』より、1982-2010年の平年値。但し、オスロと東京は、1981-2010年の平年値、ストックホルム1982-1994年の平年値
8) 可照時間・南中時太陽高度：「日の出・日の入り計算サイト」(カシオ計算機株式会社)を用いて,春分、夏至、秋分、冬至の日にて算出。

りも温暖で、冬でも不凍港があるほどである。

　アイスランド本島は北緯63度から66度に位置し、面積は日本の3割弱で、北海道よりやや大きいほどである。国土は、火山島（最高高さは2,110m）で、多くの間欠泉や温泉が見られ、世界最大の露天温泉「ブルーラグーン」で有名である。地表の約10％は氷河に覆われているが、北大西洋海流の影響を強く受けるため、冬の寒さはそれほど厳しくはなく、同緯度にあたるフィンランドやスウェーデンの北部の2月の最低気温の平均が氷点下20度近くであるのに対し、アイスランドは氷点下3度ほどである。

北欧の四季と光

　さて本書の主題である光についてであるが、北欧は高緯度に位置するゆえに独特の光の環境を有しており、季節による差異も大きい。先に記したように各国の地勢や気候は異なるが、ここでは大きく北欧全体を俯瞰して四季と光の特徴について概説する。

　北欧の長い冬は、太陽の出ている時間が短く、太陽が昇ってもその太陽高度は低く、すぐに太陽は沈む。例えば、北緯60度のオスロやヘルシンキでは、一年で日が一番短い冬至には、太陽は6時間程度しか昇らず、太陽高度は7度にも上がらない。北緯55度のデンマークコペンハーゲンでは7時間で11度、北緯65度のアイスランド・レイキャヴィークでは4時間で、太陽高度は3度にも満たない。しかもこの時期、多くの地域は天候が悪く、暗く憂鬱な日々が続き、太陽の光を希求する思いが強くなる季節である。

　春が訪れると、急速に日に日に光の量が増えて悦びの夏の季節への移行が始まる。北欧の人々は春の訪れを、気温の変化や草花の芽生えなどではなく、太陽の光の量の変化で感じると言われる。春先に残った銀色の雪面に太陽が射した時の美しさは格別である。

　そして待ちに待った夏が到来。太陽はなかなか沈まず、天候もすぐれる時期である。人々は、冬の鬱憤を晴らすかのように、夏の太陽の恩恵を受けるべく、太陽の光を存分に浴びて楽しむ。オスロやヘルシンキにおいて1年で一番日が長い夏至の時期には、朝4時頃より夜の22時頃まで太陽が出ており、太陽は一時的に地平線に沈んでも、空は白みがかかっており、完全な闇夜は訪れない。コペンハーゲンの夏至の可照時間は、17時間半、レイキャヴィークでは21時間を超える。

　至福の夏は短くすぐに秋に移行する。秋にはきれいな紅葉の時季などもあるが、冬に向けて太陽高度がどんどん下がり、日も急激に短く、空も暗くなり、すぐに次の冬へとつながっていく。

　このように夏と冬で極度に異なる真逆の環境が繰り返されるが、北欧諸国ではその連続性の中で長い時間をかけて、光に対する敏感な感覚や光を美しく扱う技法などが育まれてきたのだと思われる。

　また、太陽高度に関しては、一年で最も太陽が高くあがる夏至においても、50度前後であり、春分・秋分で30度前後、冬至については、先に示した通りほとんどの地域が10度にも満たない。このように一年を通じて低い太陽高度の光が支配し、その光が、北欧独特の美しい景観や建築内部における美しい光の空間を生み出す大きな要因となっているのである。

Climate of Nordic Countries

Topography and Climate

The five Nordic countries introduced in this book lie between latitude ~50° and 70°, including the Arctic Circle (latitude 66° and north). Despite the high latitude, the climate is relatively mild due to the North Atlantic Current, a warm current that continues from the Gulf Stream to the west coast of Europe. This section provides a brief explanation of the topography and climate in each country. The left side of the table shows land area, forested land ratio, water area ratio, etc., by country, and the right side shows average temperature, humidity, and possible sunshine duration of each season in the capital of each country.

Denmark is bordered to the south by Germany, and mainly consists of the Jutland Peninsula that continues from Germany, Funen with the ancient city of Odense, and Zealand with Copenhagen. In addition, the country has some 500 islands and its total land area is similar to that of Kyushu Island. The land is mostly flat (highest elevation: 173m) with scarce forests (forested land ratio: 11.8%). An idyllic landscape of a series of fields, mainly growing wheat, enfolds outside the urban areas, and dairy farming is also common. Since the latitude is the lowest among the five countries, its climate is the mildest. Weather changes frequently due to lack of mountains; however, rainfall is low and accumulation of snow is rare, unlike other four countries.

Sweden is the largest country among the Nordic countries by area: around 1.2 times larger than Japan. The country lies between the center and the east coast of the Scandinavian Peninsula, and borders Norway to the west, where the gently sloping Scandinavian Mountains (at about 2,000m elevation, the highest elevation of 2,104m) run in the north-south direction. On the east side, Finland is located across the Gulf of Bothnia. Sweden also borders Finland on the north part of the land. The area higher in latitude than the Arctic Circle across Finland, Sweden, Norway, and Russia, is called Lapland, where an indigenous population of the Sami people traditionally lives.

Forested land (forested land ratio: 70%) and lakes (water area ratio: 8.7%) are abundant in Sweden. There are also plains, though small. The only fertile land is in the Scania County in the south. The central and north regions are not suitable for agriculture, and dairy farming is mainly conducted.

Finland is bordered by Norway to the north and Sweden to the west, and it faces the Gulf of Bothnia to the west, the Baltic Sea to the southwest, and the Gulf of Finland to the south. Its land also borders Russia to the east and southeast. The land is mostly flat but there are some highlands in the north and northeast region (highest elevation: 1,324m). Due to having the most abundant forested land and lakes (forested land ratio: 73.9%, water area ratio: 9.4%) among the five Nordic countries, Finland is called "a country of forests and lakes".
As for the climate, the winter in Sweden and Finland is more severe compared with countries at the same latitude such as Norway and Iceland, which are directly affected by the North Atlantic Current. Many regions in the north have an average temperature of negative ten Celsius in winter, and ports and lakes are often frozen.

Norway is located on the west coast of the Scandinavian Peninsula, and its land area is about the same as Japan. Facing the Arctic Ocean and the Norwegian Sea, its coast has well developed fjords, or complicated inlets created by glacial erosion. Since a majority of its land is in the Scandinavian Mountains, there is little flat land (highest elevation: 2,469m).
The climate is strongly affected by the Norwegian Current, a branch of the North Atlantic Current, and is much warmer than Sweden and Finland, except in mountainous areas. There are some ice-free ports even in winter.

The main island of Iceland is located between 63°N and 66°N, and is a little bigger than Hokkaido. The volcanic island (highest elevation: 2,210m) has plentiful geysers and hot springs, and is famous for the world's largest geothermal spa, "Blue Lagoon". Ten percent of its land surface area is covered with glaciers, though winter is not very harsh due to the profound effect of the North Atlantic Current. The average lowest temperature in February is nearly -20 Celsius in northern Finland and Sweden at the same latitude, while it is around -3 Celsius in Iceland.

Country	National Land				Climate						Capital
	Land area (m²)	Highest elevation (m)	Forested land ratio (%)	Water area ratio (%)	Average temperature (°C)	Average relative humidity (%)	Precipitation (mm)	Possible sunshine duration (h)*	Culmination altitude of the sun (°)*	Season	
Iceland	103,000	2,110	0.50%	2.70%	0.6	77.4	82.5	12.5	26	March/vernal equinox*	Reykjavík (64.8° N)
					9.5	79	43.4	21.3	49	June/summer solstice*	
					8	79	75	12.2	26	September/autumnal equinox*	
					0.6	78.5	97	4.3	3	December/winter solstice*	
Norway	323,787	2,469	30.70%	6.00%	-5.2	80	61.7	12.3	31	March/vernal equinox*	Oslo (59.5° N)
					13.9	66	75.4	18.8	54	June/summer solstice*	
					10	79	82.2	12.2	30	September/autumnal equinox*	
					-4.6	89	62,2	6.0	7	December/winter solstice*	
Finland	338,431	1,324	73.90%	9.40%	-1.9	80	54.4	12.3	30	March/vernal equinox*	Helsinki (60.1° N)
					14.6	66	59.3	19.0	53	June/summer solstice*	
					10.7	85	65.3	12.5	30	September/autumnal equinox*	
					-3.1	93	56.9	6.8	7	December/winter solstice*	
Sweden	450,295	2,104	66.90%	8.70%	6.6	74	37.2	12.3	31	March/vernal equinox*	Stockholm (59.2° N)
					14.7	65	52.3	18.7	54	June/summer solstice*	
					11.3	78	64.7	9.7	30	September/autumnal equinox*	
					-0.8	88	44.4	8.0	7	December/winter solstice*	
Denmark	43,094	171	11.80%	1.60%	3.4	82	41.8	12.3	35	March/vernal equinox*	Copenhagen (55.4° N)
					15.6	72	60	17.5	58	June/summer solstice*	
					14	78	58.8	12.2	34	September/autumnal equinox*	
					2.5	85	48.6	7.0	11	December/winter solstice*	
Japan	377,972	3,776	68.20%	0.80%	9.4	55	117.5	12.2	55	March/vernal equinox*	Tokyo (38° N)
					22.1	72	167.7	14.7	78	June/summer solstice*	
					23.8	71	209.9	12.2	54	September/autumnal equinox*	
					8.7	52	51	9.8	31	December/winter solstice*	

1) Land area: https://en.wikipedia.org/wiki/List_of_sovereign_states_and_dependencies_by_area
2) Highest elevation: https://en.wikipedia.org/wiki/List_of_elevation_extremes_by_country
3) Forested land ratio: FAO, The Global Forest Resource Assessment 2005.
4) Water area ratio: each country's Wikipedia data
5) Average temperature: Average of 1981-2010, except Stockholm (average of 1982-1994) from Chronological Science Tables by the National Astronomical Observatory of Japan (2013, Maruzen Publishing Co., Ltd.).
6) Relative humidity: Average of 1961-1990, except Stockholm & Helsinki (1982-1967), and Tokyo (1981-2010) from Chronological Science Tables by the National Astronomical Observatory of Japan (2013, Maruzen Publishing Co., Ltd.). Copenhagen is average of 1961-1990 from Ministry of Transport Technical Report 99-5 by Danish Meteorological Institute (Copenhagen 1999).
7) Precipitation: Average of 1982-2010, except Oslo & Tokyo (1981-2010), and Stockholm (1982-1994) from Chronological Science Tables by the National Astronomical Observatory of Japan (2013, Maruzen Publishing Co., Ltd.).
8) Possible sunshine duration and culmination altitude of the sun: Calculated for equinoxes and solstices using a sunrise and sunset calculation site (Casio Computer Co., Ltd.)

Four Seasons and the Light

As for the main subject of this book, the light environment in Nordic countries is unique and largely fluctuates depending on the seasons, due to their location in a high latitude. Although the topography and climate vary in the countries as described above, this section roughly summarizes the characteristics of the four seasons and light in the overall Nordic area.

During the long Nordic winters, the duration of daytime is short, the solar elevation is low when the sun is out, and the sun sets quickly. For instance, on the winter solstice (the shortest daytime of the year), the daylight lasts only about six hours with a solar elevation of less than seven degrees in Oslo and Helsinki at 60°N, seven hours and eleven degrees in Copenhagen, Denmark at 55°N, and four hours and less than three degrees in Reykjavík, Iceland at 65°N. Furthermore, many areas have bad weather and dark, depressing days persist in this season, enhancing people's desire for sunlight.

When spring comes, the amount of light rapidly increases day by day, and transition to a joyful summer begins. It is said that Nordic people feel the arrival of spring by the change in the amount of sunlight, instead of temperature changes or budding of grasses and flowers. The beauty of sunlit, silver-colored lingering snow in early spring is exceptional.

Then, the long awaited summer comes. The daytime is long and the weather is beautiful. As if dispelling the winter displeasure, people fully enjoy the sunlight in order to receive much benefit from the summer sun. Around the summer solstice (the longest daytime of the year) in Oslo and Helsinki, the sun is out from around 4am to 10pm. The night sky is still a whitish color after the sun temporary sets below the horizon, and complete darkness never comes. The potential sunshine duration on summer solstices is 17.5 hours in Copenhagen, and beyond 21 hours in Reykjavík.

The blissful summer is short and soon transitions to the fall. Although beautiful fall colors can be enjoyed briefly, the solar elevation swiftly drops as winter comes near, daytime becomes increasingly short, the sky turns dark, and the following winter returns as usual.

The extremely different, opposite conditions are repeatedly experienced in summer and winter. In Nordic countries, keen senses of light and techniques for handling light seem to have been fostered over time through such sequences.

Furthermore, the solar elevation is only around 50 degrees on the summer solstice, when the sun reaches its highest position of the year, and around 30 degrees on vernal and autumnal equinoxesFurthermore, the solar elevation is only around 50 degrees on the summer solstice, when the sun reaches its highest position of the year, and around 30 degrees on vernal and autumnal equinoxes. The elevation on the winter solstice is less than 10 degrees in most areas, as described earlier.. The low solar elevation dominates throughout the year, and such light is a significant factor in creating unique Nordic sceneries, and beautiful light spaces in the interiors of buildings.

Examples and Map

▶ 国ごとに、教会の事例データを記載する：教会名称(Eng)／設計者(Eng)／竣工年／所在住所(各国語 または英語)、建物名称(Jpn)／設計者(Jpn)／所在都市(Jpn)、[掲載文献]
▶ 参考にした主な文献は、参考資料リストの番号 [　] にて記す。雑誌については、掲載年月を記載。
▶ 本文中図面は、参考文献をもとに作図したものである。
▶ 本文中の平面図の方位はすべてgoogle mapより特定。

Denmark

1)
Bagsvaerd Church/Jørn Utzon/1976/ Taxvej 14-16, 2880 Bagsværd (near Copenhagen)
バウスヴェア教会　ヨーン・ウッツォン／バウスヴェア（コペンハーゲン近郊）
[2] [3] [4] [5] [6] [8] [11] [15] [16] [17] [20] [21] [26] [DK.1982.3]

2)
Grundtvigs Church P.V.Jensen Klint/Kaare Klint/1940/ På Bjerget 14B, 2400 Copenhagen
グルントヴィ教会　PVイェンセン・クリント、コーレ・クリント／コペンハーゲン
[5] [7] [11] [13] [14] [16] [17] [22]

3)
Islev Church/Inger & Johannes Exner/1970/ Slotsherrensvej 321, 2610 Rødovre (near Copenhagen)
イスレブ教会／インガー＆ヨハネス・エクスナー／ロツオウレ、（コペンハーゲン近郊）
[4] [5] [21] [DK.1973.5]

4)
Gug Church/Inger & Johannes Exner/1972/Nøhr Sørensens Vej 7　9210 Aalborg
グウ教会／インガー＆ヨハネス・エクスナー／オールボー
[4] [5] [20] [21] [DK.1975.4, 1994.1]

5)
Enghøj Church/Henning Larsen/1994/ Enghøj Alle 10, 8920 Randers
エンホイ教会／ヘニング・ラーセン／ランナース
[5] [8] [11] [15] [21] [27]

6)
Aarhus Chapel Crematorium/Henning Larsen/1967/Viborgvej 47A, 8210 Aarhus
オーフス火葬場の礼拝堂／ヘニング・ラーセン／オーフス
[5] [21] [DK.1972.5]

7)
Egedal Church/Fogh & Følner/1990/Egedalsvej 3, 2980 Kokkedal (near Copenhagen)
エーエダル教会／フォウ＆フェルナー／コケダル（コペンハーゲン近郊）
[15] [21] [DK.1994.3]

8)
Sankt Clemens Church/Inger & Johannes Exner, Knud Erik Larsen/1963/ Parkboulevarden 15, 8900 Randers
聖クレメンス教会／インガー＆ヨハネス・エクスナー, クヌツ・エーリク・ラーセン／ランナース
[5] [21] [DK.1964.3]

9)
Tornbjerg Church/Fogh & Følner/1994/ Skærmhatten 1, 5220 Odense
トーンビア教会／フォウ＆フェルナー／オーデンセ
[8] [15] [21]

10)
Church of the Resurrection/Inger & Johannes Exner/1984/Gymnasievej 2, 2620 Albertslund (near Copenhagen)／復活教会／インガー＆ヨハネス・エクスナー／アルベアツルン（コペンハーゲン近郊）
[5] [21] [DK.1988.3]

11)
Dybkær Church/Regnbuen Arkitekter/2010/ Arendalsvej 1-9, 8600 Silkeborg
デュブケア教会／ラインブーエン建築設計事務所／シルケボー
[5] [11]

12)
Antvorskov Church/Regnbuen Arkitekter/2005/ Agersøvej 86B, 4200 Slagelse
アントヴォスコウ教会／ラインブーエン建築設計事務所／スラーエルセ
[5]

Sweden

1)
The Woodland Cemetery/Erik Gunnar Asplund/1940/Sockenvägen, 122 33 Stockholm
森の火葬場／グンナール・アスプルンド／ストックホルム
[4] [7] [11] [12] [13] [14] [16] [18] [20] [29] [30] [31] [32]

2)
The Woodland Chapel/Erik Gunnar Asplund/1920/ Sockenvägen, 122 33 Stockholm
森の礼拝堂／グンナール・アスプルンド／ストックホルム
[4] [7] [11] [12] [13] [14] [16] [18] [20] [22] [29] [31] [32]

3)
Chapel of Resnrrection/Sigurd Lewerentz/1925/ Sockenvägen, 122 33 Stockholm
復活礼拝堂／シーグルド・レヴェレンツ／ストックホルム
[4] [5] [7] [11] [16] [20] [22] [33]

4)
Chapels of St. Knut and St. Gertrud/Sigurd Lewerentz/1943, 1955/ Scheelegatan 17, 213 64 Malmö
聖クヌット・聖ゲアトルド礼拝堂／シーグルド・レヴェレンツ／マルメ
[4] [5] [7] [16] [22] [33]

5)
St. Mark's Church/Sigurd Lewerentz/1960/ Malmovagen 51 Bjorkhagen Stockholm
聖マーク教会／シーグルド・レヴェレンツ／ストックホルム
[6] [11] [16] [18] [19] [22] [33]

6)
Church of St. Peter/Sigurd Lewerentz/1966/ Vedbyvägen, 264 21 Klippan
聖ペーター教会／シーグルド・レヴェレンツ／クリッパン
[4] [5] [6] [11] [16] [20] [22] [33] [34]

7)
Härlanda Church/Peter Celsing/1959/ Härlandavägen 23, 416 72 Göteborg
ハーランダ教会／ペーター・セルシング／ヨーテボリ
[4] [5] [11] [20] [22] [35] [36]

8)
St. Thomas Church/Peter Celsing/1959/ Kirunagatan 9, 162 68 Vällingby (near Stockholm)
聖トーマス教会　ペーター・セルシング／ヴェリンビュー（ストックホルム近郊）
[6] [16] [20] [35] [36]

9)
Almtuna Church/Peter Celsing/1959/753 26 Uppsala
アルムトゥーマ教会／ペーター・セルシング／ウプサラ
[35] [36]

10)
Olaus Petri Church/Peter Celsing/1959/ Armfeltsgatan 2, 115 34 Stockholm
オーラス・ペトリ教会／ペーター・セルシング／ストックホルム
[35] [36]

11)
Nacksta Church/Peter Celsing/1969/Vinkltået16, 85353 Sundsvall
ナクスタ教会／ペーター・セルシング／スンスヴァル
[11] [22] [35] [36]

12)
Årsta Church/Johan Celsing/2008/
Bråviksvägen 47, 120 52 Årsta (near Stockholm)
オースタ教会／ヨハン・セルシング／オースタ（ストックホルム近郊）
[AR2012.1] [AU. 2016.4]

13)
Farsta Församling Söderleds Church/Borgström and Lindroos/1960/ Lingvägen 149, 123 59 Farsta (near Stockholm)
ファースタ・フォサムリン・ソーダレツ教会／ボリストロム＆リンドロース／ファースタ（ストックホルム近郊）
[20]

Finland
1)
Chapel of the Resurrection/Erik Bryggman/1941/ Hautausmaantie 21, Turku
復活礼拝堂／エリック・ブリュッグマン／トゥルク
[1] [4] [7] [10] [11] [16] [20] [23] [24] [40] [AA.1942.07, 1942.08, 1984.07]

2)
Mänistö Church/Juha Leiviskä/1992/
8, Kellolahdentie, 70460 Kuopio
マンニスト教会／ユハ・レイヴィスカ／クオピオ
[5] [10] [11] [15] [23] [24] [43] [44] [45] [46] [AA.1993.02]

3)
Vuoksenniska Church/Alvar Aalto/1958/
Ruokolahdentie 27, Imatra
ヴォクセンニスカ教会／アルヴァル・アールト／1958／イマトラ
[1] [2] [3] [4] [5] [6] [10] [11] [13] [16] [20] [24] [37] [38] [39] [AA.1959.12]

4)
Nakkila Parish Church/ Erkki Huttunen/ 1937/ Kirkkokatu 4, Nakkila
ナッキラ教会／エルッキ・フットゥネン／ナッキラ
[1] [7] [15] [23] [24] [AA.1938]

5)
Otaniemi Chapel/Kaija and Heikki Siren/1957/ Jämeräntaival 8 A, Espoo (near Helsinki)
オタニエミ礼拝堂／カイヤ＆ヘイッキ・シレーン／エスポー（ヘルシンキ近郊）
[1] [4] [5] [6] [10] [11] [16] [20] [24] [41] [AA.1954.05]

6)
St. HenryÅfs Ecumenical Art Chapel/Matti Sanaksenaho/2005/ Seiskarinkatu 32, Turku
聖ヘンリ・エキュメニカル礼拝堂／マッティ・サナクセンアホ／トゥルク
[1] [5] [9] [10] [11] [AU.2006.8] [FA.2006.0405]

7)
Viikki Church / JKMM Architects/ 2005/ Agronominkatu 5, Helsinki
ヴィーッキ教会／JKMM アーキテクツ／ヘルシンキ
[1] [5] [FA.2006.0405]

8)
Kärsämäki Church/ Lassila Hirvilammi Architects, Anssi Lassila/ 2004/ Pappilankuja24, 86710 Kärsämäki
カルサマキ教会／ラッシラ・ヒルヴィランミ・アーキテクツ、アンシ・ラッシラ／カルサマキ
[1] [8] [9] [AU. 2006.8] [FA.2006.0405]

9)
Temppeliaukio Church/ Timo and Tuomo Suomalainen/ 1969 /Lutherinkatu 3, Helsinki
テンペリアウキオ教会／ティモ＆トゥオモ・スオマライネン／ヘルシンキ
[1] [4] [5] [6] [10] [11] [16] [24] [AA.1970.04]

10)
Kaleva Church/Raili and Reima Pietilä/ 1966/
Liisanpuisto 1, Tampere
カレヴァ教会／ライリ＆レイマ・ピエティラ／タンペレ
[1] [4] [5] [6] [10] [11] [16] [20] [23] [24] [42] [AA.1959.09]

11)
Malmi Church / Kristian Gullichsen/ 1980/ Kunnantie 1, Helsinki
マルミ教会／クリスティアン・グリクセン／ヘルシンキ
[1] [AA.1983.04]

12)
Kamppi Chapel of Silence/K2S Architects, 2012, Simonkatu 7, 00100 Helsinki
静粛の礼拝堂／K2S／ヘルシンキ
[AA.2012.03]

13)
Harju Funeral Chapel Renovation and Extention/ Juha Leiviskä/1998/ Saattotie 7　50120 Mikkeli
ハルユ葬儀礼拝堂改修・増築工事／ユハ・レイヴィスカ／ミッケリ
[44] [AU.1999.8]

14)
Kuokkala Church/Lassila Hirvilamm,Anssi Lassila/2008,　Syöttäjänkatu 4, Jyväskylä
クオッカラ教会　ラッシラ・ヒルヴィランミ・アーキテクト、アンシ・ラッシラ／ユヴァスキュラ
[11] [AU.2011.07] [AA.2010.04]

15)
Chapel of St. Lawrence/Avanto Architects/2011/ Pappilankuja 3, 0150, Vantaa
聖ローレンス教会／アヴァント・アーキテクツ／ヴァンター（ヘルシンキ近郊）
[AU.2011.12] [AA.2010.06]

16)
Vatiala Funerary Chapel/ Viljo Revell/ 1960/ Kappelinkierto 3, Kangasala (near Tampere)
ヴァティアラ礼拝堂／ヴィルヨ・レヴェル／カンガサラ（タンペレ近郊）
[1] [10] [23] [24] [AA.1962.05]

17)
Pirkkala Church/Käpy and Simo Paavilainen/1994/ Perkiöntie 40, 33960 Pirkkala (nearTampere)
ピルッカラ教会　キャプ＆シモ・パーヴィライネン／ピルッカラ（タンペレ近郊）
[5] [AA.1999.01]

Norway
1)
St. Hallvard's Church and Monastery/Lund and Slaatto/1966/ Enerhauggata 4, 0651 Oslo
聖ハルヴェード教会および修道院／ルンド＆スラット／オスロ
[5] [6] [16] [20] [47]

2)
Mortensrud Church/Jensen & Skodvin Arkitektkontor/2002/
Helga Vaneks Vei 15, 1281 Oslo
モルテンスルッド教会／イェンセン＆スコドヴィン設計事務所／オスロ
[6] [9] [11] [16] [19] [AU.2002.08]

3)
Bøler Church/Hansen-Bjørndal Arkitekter/2004/ General Ruges vei 51, 0691 Oslo
ボゥーラー教会／ハンセン・ビョルンダール設計事務所／2004年／オスロ
[5]

4)
Vardåsen Church/Terje Grønmo/2003/Vardefaret 40, 1388 Borgen, Asker (near Oslo)
ヴァードオーセン教会／テァイェ・グロンモ／2003年／アスカー（オスロ近郊）
[5]

5)
Tautra Mariakloster/Jensen & Skodvin Arkitektkontor/2006/ Tautra Mariakloster, bakken norde, 7633 Frosta
タウトラ・マリア修道院／イェンセン＆スコドヴィン設計事務所／タウトラ
[9] [11] [25] [DT.2008.11]

6)
Brumunddal Church /Molle & Per Cappelen/1965/ Kikevegen 67ー, 2380 Brumunddal

ブルムンダール教会／モレ＆ペア・カペレン／ブルムンダール
[5]

7)
St. Magnus Church /Lund and Slaatto/ 1988/ Romeriksgata 1, 2003 Lillestrøm
聖マウヌス教会／ルンド＆スラット／リレストルム
[5] [6]

8)
Knarvik Church/Reiulf Ramstad Architects/2015/ Kvernhushaugane 19, 5914 Isdalstø (near Bergen)
クナーヴィク教会／レイウルフ・ラムスタッド設計事務所／イスダルスト（ベルゲン近郊）
http://www.archdaily.com/574811/community-church-knarvik-reiulf-ramstad-arkitekter

9)
Arctic Cathedral/Jan Inge Hovig/1965/ Hans Nilsens vei 41, 9020 Tromsdalen
北極教会／ヤン・インゲ・ホービ／トロムソ
[16]
https://en.wikipedia.org/wiki/Arctic_Cathedral

Iceland
1)
Neskirkja Church/Águst Pálsson/1957/ Hagatorg, 107 Reykjavík,
ネス教会／アウグスト・パルソン／レイキャヴィーク
https://tripcreator.com/iceland/item/5b2e9d8e-ac3d-4f3a-9331-3a5425c543f2/neskirkja-church

2)
Hallgrimskirkja Church/Guðjón Samúelsson/ 1940-74/Hallgrímstorg 101, Reykjavík,
ハルグリム教会／グドジョン・サムエルソン／レイキャヴィーク
[15]
https://en.wikipedia.org/wiki/Hallgr%C3%ADmskirkja

References

▶ 光の空間・デザイン

[1] フィンランド光の旅 北欧建築探訪、小泉 隆 プチグラパブリッシング、2009
[2] アルヴァル・アールト 光と建築、小泉 隆 プチグラパブリッシング、2013
[3] 光の建築を読み解く、日本建築学会編（中村芳樹、吉澤望、坂本卓、小泉隆ほか）、彰国社、2015
[4] マスターズ・オヴ・ライト（1）20世紀のパイオニアたち、ヘンリー・プラマー、株式会社エー・アンド・ユー、2003
[5] Nordic Light: Modern Scandinavian Architecture、Henry Plummer、Thames & Hudson、2014

▶ 教会建築

[6] Architectural Guide: Christian Sacred Buildings in Europe Since 1950, Wolfgang Jean Stock, Prestel, 2004
[7] European Church Architecture 1900-1950, Wolfgang Jean Stock, Prestel, 2006
[8] A Design Manual Sacred Buildings, Rudolf Stegers, Birkhäuser, 2008
[9] Closer to God: Religious Architecture and Sacred Spaces, Robert Klanten, Lukas Feireiss, Die Gestalten Verlag,2010
[10] Sacral Space Modern Finnish Churches, Jetsonen & Jetsonen, Rakennustieto, 2003

▶ 北欧の建築・デザイン

[11] 北欧の建築 エレメント＆ディテール、小泉隆、学芸出版社、2017
[12] 北欧の巨匠に学ぶデザイン アスプルンド／アールト／ヤコブセン、鈴木敏彦、杉原有紀、彰国社、2013
[13] 北欧の建築、ステーン・エイラル・ラスムッセン、吉田 鉄郎（翻訳）、鹿島出版会、1978
[14] 図説 北欧の建築遺産、伊藤 大介、河出書房新社、2010
[15] ヨーロッパ建築案内〈3〉、淵上 正幸、TOTO出版、2001
[16] 世界の建築・街並みガイド2 イギリス／アイルランド／北欧4国、渡邉 研司、松本 淳、北川 卓、エクスナレッジ、2003
[17] デンマーク デザインの国―豊かな暮らしを創る人と造形、島崎信、学芸出版社、2003
[18] ストックホルムの建築（建築巡礼）、小川 信子、外山 義、丸善、1991
[19] ノルウェーのデザイン―美しい風土と優れた家具・インテリア・グラフィックデザイン、島崎 信、誠文堂新光社、2007
[20] Nordic Architecture, Nils-Ole Lund, Arkitektens Forlag, 2008
[21] Danish Architecture 1960-1995, Kim Dirkinck- Holmfeld, Arkitektens Forlag, 1995
[22] A guide to Swedish architecture, The Swedish Institute, 2001
[23] A Guide to Finnish Architecture, Jouni Kaipia & Lauri Putkonen, Otava, 1997
[24] 20th-Century Architecture Finland, Marja-Riitta Norri, Elina Standertskjöld, Wilfried Wang, Museum of Finnish Architecture, 2000
[25] Made in Norway: Norwegian Architecture Today、Ingerid Helsing Almaas（editor）、Birkhäuser、2010

▶ 個別の建築家あるいは建築

[26] Jorn Utzon: Drawings and Buildings, Michael Asgaard Andersen, Princeton Architectural Press, 2013
[27] Henning Larsen: The Architect's Studio, Kjeld Vindum, Louisiana , 2002
[28] PV. Jensen-Klint, Thomas Bo Jensen , Routledge, 2009
[29] アスプルンドの建築―北欧近代建築の黎明、スチュアート・レーデ（著）、樋口 清（訳）、武藤 章（訳）、鹿島出版会 1982
[30] E.G.アスプルンド（現代の建築家）、E.G.アスプルンド（著）、鹿島出版会、1983
[31] アスプルンドの建築 1885-1940、川島 洋一（著）、吉村行雄（写真）、TOTO出版、2005
[32] ASPLUND, Claes Caldenby & Olof Hultin , Gingko press, 1997
[33] Sigurd Lewerenttz 1885-1975（Electa architecture）, Nicola flora, Phaidon Press. 2002
[34] St. Petri: Klippan 1962-66（O'Neil Ford Monograph）,Sigurd Lewerentz,Ernst Wasmuth Verlag ,2009
[35] PETER SELCING: The Façade is the Meeting between Outside and inside（Five Masters of the North），Museum of Finnish Architecture,1992
[36] The Architecture of Peter Celsing, Wilfried Wang, Arvinius Forlag, 1997
[37] アルヴァ・アアルト、武藤章、鹿島出版会、1969
[38] ALVAR AALTO, Volume I〜III of the Complete Works, Birkhauser, 1963, 1971
[39] Alvar Aalto: The Complete Catalogue of Architecture, Design & Art（World cities series）G. Schildt , Wiley,1978
[40] ERIK BRYGGMAN 1891-1955 architect, Museum of Finnish Architecture,1991
[41] Kaija+ Heikki Siren, Otava, 1976
[42] PIETILÄ intermediate zones in modern architecture, Museum of Finnish Architecture, Alvar Aalto Museum, 1985
[43] Juha Leiviskä, Museum of Finnish Architecture, 1999
[44] Juha Leiviskä and the Continuity of Finnish Modern Architecture, Malcolm Quantrill, Wiley- Academy, 2001
[45] 特集 ユハ・レイヴィスカ、a+u、（株）エー・アンド・ユー、1991年7月号、1995年4月号
[46] TRANSPARENT WALL Works by Markku Pääkkönen, Alvar Aalto Academy, 2004
[47] Lund & Slaatto ST. HALLVARD KIRKE OG KIOSTER, Jiri Havran (foto), Christian Norberg- Schulz, Kjell Lund, etc, ARFO, 1992

▶ 雑誌

[DK] ArkiteKtur DK, Arkitektens Forlag / The Danish Architectural Press
[AA] ark ARKKITEHTI/ The Finnish Architectural Review, Suomen Arkkitehtiliitto SAFA/Finnish Association of Architect
[FA] Finnish Architecture, Alvar Aalto Academy, Finnish Association of Architects, Museum of Finnish Architecture
[AR] The Architectural Review, EMAP Publishing Limited
[AU] a+u、（株）エー・アンド・ユー
[DT] DETAIL, Detail publishers

あとがき

「人は記述されたものから決して芸術を経験することは出来ない。説明と分析とは、せいぜい予備知識の提供だけである。しかし、それらは人に実際の芸術作品を体験しよう、という気をおこさせるに違いない」
　　ラズラ・モホリ＝ナギ「素材から建築へ」より
（The New Vision）(1927) [1]

　美しい光の空間を求めて北の地へ足を運ぶようになり十数年になるが、これまでに『フィンランド光の旅　北欧建築探訪』[2]、『アルヴァル・アールト　光と建築』[3]、そして本書『北欧モダンチャーチ＆チャペル　聖なる光と祈りの空間』と、光をテーマにしながら北欧の建築を紹介する書籍を刊行させていただいた。
　これらに共通する大きな意図は、北欧の素晴らしい建築に足を運んでいただき、その良さを知って欲しいことである。饒舌でない、あえて語ろうとしないことも多い北欧建築の良さは、写真や解説などでは伝わりにくく、実際に体験しないとわからないことが多いからだ。
　本書も含め、これまでに紹介している北欧の建築や私が現代において良き参考例にすべきと思う建築は、その土地の風土や歴史との連続性を保ちながら、長い時間愛され、使い続けられながら、日常において豊かさや美しさ、そして悦びを与えている建築である。このような建築の在り方は、いつの時代も大切にしなければいけないのではないか。特に次から次へと新しい建築が生まれては消費されてしまう現代においては、改めてそのことを認識する必要があるとの思いにかられる。
　本書では、光と空間が素晴らしいことを事例選定の第一義の視点としながら、建築の在り方として望ましいと思われるものを取り上げたが、国によって状況も異なり、選定した事例群を振り返り少し補足をしたい。

　デンマークについては、シドニー・オペラハウスの設計で著名な建築家ヨーン・ウッツォン (1918-2008) によるバウスヴェア教会、観光名所として挙げられることも多いグルントヴィ教会、「光の巨匠」とも呼ばれる建築家ヘニング・ラーセン (1925-2013) によるエンホイ教会を取り上げているが、その他の教会については日本ではあまり知られていない建築がほとんどかもしれない。インガー＆ヨハネス・エクスナーは、デンマークで数多くの教会を作っている建築家であるが、ユニークな特徴を持つものも多い。各地方に点在するそれらの教会は、伝統的な煉瓦造教会との連続性を保ちながらも、現代的で洗練され、気品に満ちた空間が多い。そしてどの教会も、地域の人々のコミュニティの場として愛され使われている感覚を現地で強く感じた。

　スウェーデンについては、グンナール・アスプルンド (1885-1940)、シーグルド・レヴェレンツ (1885-1975)、ペーター・セルシング (1920-1974) というスウェーデンの3人の巨匠建築家が教会堂、礼拝堂を多く作っていることもあり、それらの作品を中心に取り上げることにした。
　世界遺産にも登録されているアスプルンドによる森の火葬場は、アスプルンドの最後の作品であるが、生と死に向き合う人間の精神に働きかけるその空間は秀逸である。アスプルンドと同時代のシーグルド・レヴェレンツの教会には、考え抜かれた素材やディテールそして抑制された光を用いて暗さの中に独特の神秘性を生み出している作品が多い。ペーター・セルシングは、日本では馴染みのうすい建築家かもしれないが、アスプルンド、レ

ヴェレンツの流れをくみ、光、素材、プロポーションの取り扱いにたけた建築家である。そして現在のスウェーデン建築界で活躍するその息子のヨハン・セルシング (1955-) の作品も取り上げた。最後に掲載したステンドグラスの美しいフォースタ教会は、北欧建築の名作としてしばしば紹介されるものである。

フィンランドは、北欧諸国の中で最も多く良質な教会建築がある国と思われる。世界的な近代建築の巨匠アルヴァル・アールト (1898-1976) の存在が大きく、アールトの時代およびそれ以降のフィンランド建築界の充実さや建築家の層の厚みの表れと取ることもできる。今回とりあげた事例は、前書『フィンランド光の旅　北欧建築探訪』の中より代表的なものを再録し、その後、新たに調査をした事例などを加えて編成した。本書収録の事例以外にも沢山良い教会があるので、ぜひとも前書についてもご覧いただければと思う。フィンランドの教会建築は多様であるが、国の豊富な資源である木材を用いた例が多いこと、森や地盤などの自然との共生の感覚が多分にあること、明るさへの希求の表れでもある白い空間が多いこと、礼拝の場というよりも生活空間の延長のように思えることさえある自由な感覚が見られることなどが興味深い。

ノルウェーの建築自体、日本では馴染みがうすいかもしれないが、近現代建築において代表的な教会として挙げられることが多いルンド＆スラットによる聖ハルヴェード教会と若手建築家のイェンセン＆スコドヴィン設計事務所によるモーテンスルッド教会、またイェンセン＆スコドヴィンによる最近の作品タウトラの修道院を取り上げた。

タウトラ・マリア修道院については、夜明け前のお祈りから就寝前の1日7回の祈りの時間にじっくりと立ち会うことが出来た。厳格な戒律で知られるシトー派修道院の厳正な雰囲気の中、ノルウェー的な感覚といえるのか、建築家の個性なのか、木々や水面そして空や光などの自然要素との共生の感覚や明るさや軽さの感覚との共存が興味深く、周囲の景観の美しさもあって多くの頁を割くことになった。また森の中に何世紀も前からそこにあったような佇まいを見せていた柿葺きのブルムンダール教会も印象深い。その他にも現代的で良質な教会が多く建てられている。なおノルウェー建築界を代表する建築家スヴェレ・フェーン (1924-2008) については、教会の実作がない。

さて、アイスランドや北緯66度以北の北極圏にまであがると、ノルウェー・トロムソの北極教会、アイスランドのハルグリム教会などが観光名所としても名高いが、それらは内部空間よりも、厳しい自然と対峙する力強い外観に大きな特徴が見いだせる。

これら各事例の解説に際しては、これまでの優れた研究者らによる研究書や書籍などを参考に、そこに自分の空間体験を重ね合わせ、読者にできるだけ空間の質や空間体験をわかりやすく伝え、興味を持っていただけるよう心がけた。

教会だけではないが、旅をする楽しみの一つとして、現地で出会う人との接触があげられよう。教会関係者の方々は、見学に際して本当に快く、日本からの訪問を歓

迎してくれた。そして誇りを持って自分達の教会を紹介してくれる。このことは教会が日頃より愛され使用されていることを物語る。たどり着くのに難しい教会では、現地までの交通の手配をして頂いたりもした。教会に学びに来た学生や子供達も、優しく微笑んで日本からの私に声をかけてくれる。

　撮影や空間との接しかたについては、日頃より、どれだけ豊かな瞬間に出会えるかを大切にしている。そのため、教会の最も美しくなる瞬間を求めて季節時刻天候を見定め撮影をすることも多いのであるが、デンマークのある教会で「この教会はいつが一番美しいですか」と関係者に尋ねたところ「そこにはいつも常に美があります。あなた次第です」との言葉に教えられた気がした。

謝辞
　本書が出来上がるまでに多くの人にお世話になった。まずは現地で見学をさせて頂いたすべての教会関係者に感謝の意を表したい。そして教会までの道程の手配までして頂き、貴重な体験の機会を与えてくれたタウトラ・マリア修道院のシェリル・チェン (Sr. Sheryl Chen) さん、改修中にも関わらず見学の便宜を図ってくれ、道中でもお世話になったクナーヴィク教会のヴェロニカ・オーラフセン・ロラン (Weronica Olafsen Løland) さんには、特に厚く御礼を申し上げたい。

　本の編集・作成にあたっては、日本語読みの監修でお世話になったリセ・スコウ (Lise Schou) さん、坂根シルック (Sakane Sirkku) さん、また限られたい時間の中で作図をして頂いた井形寛さんとその協力者に心より感謝いたします。

　そしてバナナブックスの石原秀一編集長には、この企画の価値を認めて頂き、本の完成までに大変お世話になり深くお礼を申し上げます。

　最後に、多くの現地調査に辛抱強く同行し、編集作業などでも協力を得た妻・智子に改めて感謝したい。そして最後に、敬虔なクリスチャンであった亡き母 敏子に本書が届くことを願って筆を置かせて頂きます。

2017年11月　小泉 隆

1）この引用文は、ミカエル・トレンチャー著の『建築ガイドブックアルヴァー・アアルト（平山達訳、丸善、2009）の序論でも紹介されている。
　 The ALAVAR AALTO Guide, Michael Trencher,Princeton Architectural Press, 1996
2）小泉隆「フィンランド 光の旅　北欧建築探訪」（プチグラパブリッシング、2009）、
3）小泉隆「アルヴァル・アールト　光と建築」（プチグラパブリッシング、2013）

Postscript

"One can never experience art through descriptions. Explanations and analysis can serve at best as intellectual preparation. They may, however, encourage one to make direct contact with works of art."
Laszlo Moholy-Nagy, From Material to Architecture (The New Vision) (1927)1

It has been about a dozen years since I began to visit the northland in pursuit of beautiful light spaces, and I have published books to introduce Nordic architecture: "Light Space in Finland", "Alvar Aalto: Light and Architecture", and this book, "Nordic Modern Church & Chapel Light in the Sacred Space".
My overall desire shared in these books is for people to actually visit the superb Nordic architecture, and recognize its virtue. The virtue of the non-overtalkative and often taciturn Nordic architecture is hard to understand through photos and descriptions, and many things cannot be absorbed without experiencing them in real life.

The Nordic architecture I have introduced, including the works in this book, and the architecture that should be used as a reference, in my opinion, are the ones that retain a connection with the climate and history of the land, that are cherished and used long term, and that provide abundance, beauty, and joy in everyday life. I cannot help thinking that such a way of architecture should be valued regardless of the era, and this should be reacknowledged particularly in the modern age where new buildings are made and consumed one after another.

While superiority of light and space are the first perspective in selecting example architecture for this book, I introduced examples in which the appearance as architecture is considered to be desirable. Since the circumstances differ in each country, I would like look back on the selected examples and give additional explanations.

For Denmark, the examples included: Bagsvaerd Church, designed by architect Jorn Utzon (1918-2008), who is famous for the Sydney Opera House design; Grundtvigs Church, that is often listed as a sightseeing spot; and Enghøl Church by Henning Larsen (1925-2013), who is known as the "master of light". However, the other examples might not be well known in Japan. Inger & Johannes Exner are an architect couple who designed numerous church buildings, and many of their designs have unique characteristics. In the churches scattered in local areas, modern and sophisticated spaces with elegance are made, while maintaining connections with traditional brick construction churches. When I visited there, I felt a strong sense that each church is loved and used as a place for local communication.

For Sweden, the works of three giant architects, Gunnar Asplund (1885-1940), Sigurd Lewerentz (1885-1975), and Peter Celsing (1920-1974) are mainly introduced, as they had designed many church buildings and chapels. The Woodland Cemetery, listed as a World Heritage site, is the last work of Asplund. The space, drawing on the human mentality of confronting life and death, is splendid. Sigurd Lewerentz lived in the same era as Asplund, and his works include many crematoriums and church buildings. By consideration of materials and details, and using suppressed light, many of his works create a unique mystique in the darkness. Peter Celsing may not be well known in Japan, but he is reminiscent of Asplund and Lewerentz, and was good at handling light, materials, and proportions. A work of his son who is an active architect in Sweden today, Johan Celsing (1955-), was also included. The last example, Farsta Church with its superb stained glass, is often introduced as a masterpiece of Nordic architecture.

Finland is perhaps the country where the largest number of good quality church architecture exists among the Nordic countries. This is largely due to the world-famous, modern architectural legend Alvar Aalto (1898-1976). It also could be a representation of the fulfillment of the Finnish architectural industry since Aalto, and the abundance of a wide range of architects. The examples in this book include the representative works introduced in my former book, "Light Space in Finland", as well as works that were subsequently examined. I would be happy if the readers would take a look at my former book, since it introduced a number of high-quality churches that were not in this book. Though the church architecture in Finland is diversified, there are several interesting points: there are many churches using wood, the country's abundant resource; there is a great feeling of living in good harmony with the natural elements such as forests and the earth; there are many white spaces, which represents a desire for light; and there is sometimes an unconstrained taste, which can make a space seem like an extension of a living space rather than a church.

Norwegian church architecture (perhaps it is not yet well known in Japan) included: a representative modern architecture, St. Hallvard's Church and Monastery, by Lund and Slaatto; the Mortensrud Church by a design firm of young architects, Jensen & Skodvin Arkitektkontor; and the Tautra Mariakloster, a recent work of Jensen & Skodvin Arkitektkontor. At the Tautra Mariakloster, I could carefully witness seven daily prayer times from the predawn to before bed. In a solemn atmosphere of the Cistercian abbey, known for its strict precepts, I was intrigued by the co-occurrence of the feeling of a coexistence with the natural elements (such as trees, water, sky, and light) and the feeling of brightness and lightness, but I was not sure this could be said to be a Norwegian taste, or just an identity of the architect. Combined with the scenic beauty of the surroundings, many pages are spent on this abbey. Brumunddal Church with its shingled roof left me with a strong impression, and it stood in a forest as if it was there for centuries. More modern churches are being built. A representative Norwegian architect, Sverre Fehn (1924–2009), did not leave any church works that were actually built.

In Iceland and the Arctic Circle (latitude 65° and north), the Arctic Cathedral in Tromsø, Norway and the Hallgrimskirkja Church in Iceland are famous as sightseeing spots. Their major characteristics are found in the powerful exterior appearances, confronting the harsh natural environment, rather than in the interior spaces.

With references from the research papers and books by excellent researchers in the past, combined with my personal experience of the spaces, I did my best to clearly explain the quality of the spaces and the spatial experiences, and to interest the readers. Provision of new facts or development of my own theories are not the purpose of this book.

One of the pleasures of traveling, not only to churches, is communication with people one encounters at each site. People involved in the church truly and willingly welcomed a visitor from Japan, and explained their church with pride. This shows that the church architecture is cherished and used on a regular basis. For churches with poor accessibility, I sometimes requested to have transportation arranged to a site. People visiting the church, including students and children, talked to me, a traveler from Japan, with friendly smiles.
In regard to the method of taking photos and treating a space, I always highly value how often I can encounter a moment of abundance. Therefore, I often take photographs by pinpointing a season, time, and weather in seeking the most beautiful moment of a church. However, I felt enlightened when I asked a person involved in a church in Denmark, "When is the most beautiful moment for this church?", and I was given an answer: "There is always beauty. It's up to you."

I was supported by many people in the course of making this book.
Firstly, I would like to thank all people involved in the churches that I visited. I would like to express my special appreciation for Sr. Sheryl Chen of the Tautra Mariakloster, who arranged a travel route to the church and gave precious opportunities for experiences, and Weronica Olafsen Løland of the Knarvik Church, who arranged a tour for me despite ongoing renovation work, and assisted me during travel.
For editing and making this book, I sincerely appreciate Lise Schou and Sirkku Sakane, who oversaw transliteration into the Japanese language, and Hiroshi Igata, who provided support in drawing figures regardless of his limited time.
I also would like to express my deep appreciation to Shuichi Ishihara, the chief editor of Banana Books, for recognizing the value of this project, and providing support for making the book.
 appreciate my wife Tomoko, who patiently accompanied me on many field trips, and supported editing work, as with my previous books. Finally, I would like to devote this book to Toshiko, my late mother and a devout Christian.
November 2017, Takashi KOIZUMI

1) The same quotation was used in the introduction of "The ALVAR AALTO Guide" by Michael Trencher (Princeton Architectural Press, 1996).
2) Takashi Koizumi, "Light Space in Finland", Petit Grand Publishing, 2009.
3) Takashi Koizumi, "Alvar Aalto: Light and Architecture", Petit Grand Publishing, 2013.

Nordic Modern Church & Chapel
Light in the Sacred Space

著者｜小泉　隆
九州産業大学建築都市工学部住居・インテリア学科教授、博士（工学）
1964年2月3日神奈川県横須賀市生まれ、1987年東京理科大学工学部建築学科卒業、1989年同大学院修了、1989年〜同助手、1999年より九州産業大学工学部建築学科、2010年4月より同工学部住居・インテリア学科教授。2006年度ヘルシンキ工科大学建築学科訪問研究員、2017年改組して現職

主な著書：
『北欧の建築　エレメント＆ディティール』（学芸出版社、2017）、『アルヴァル・アールト　光と建築』（プチグラパブリッシング、2013）、『フィンランド　光の旅　北欧建築探訪』（プチグラパブリッシング、2009）、『大谷採石場　不思議な地下空間』（随想舎、2010）

写真・執筆｜小泉 隆 ©
編集｜石原秀一
翻訳｜牧尾晴喜［フレーズクレーズ］
　　　ガンター倫子　ケネス・ガンター
作図｜井形 寛［かぶとむし］
作図協力｜藤下輝雄、牛尾彰吾、稲垣聖矢、西村彩花
日本語読み監修｜リセ・スコウ、坂根シルック
デザイン｜マルプデザイン
印刷・製本｜上野印刷株式会社
制作協力｜シェリル・チェン（タウトラ・マリア修道院）
　　　　　ヴェロニカ・オーラフセン・ロラン
　　　　　（クナーヴィク教会）

Author｜Takashi koizumi
Professor, Dept. of Housing and Interior Design, Faculty of Architecture and Civil Engineering, Kyushu Sangyo University; PhD (Engineering, Tokyo University of Science, 1999)
Born 3 Feb. 1964, Yokosuka, Kanagawa, Japan.
1987, BSc (Architecture), Tokyo University of Science.
1989, MSc (Architecture), Tokyo University of Science.
1989–99, Research Assistant, Dept. of Architecture, Science University of Tokyo.
1999 to present, Kyushu Sangyo University (appointed professor 2008).
2006 (academic year), guest researcher at Dept. of Architecture, Helsinki University of Technology

Publications:
Nordic Architecture Elements & Details(Gakugei Shuppansha, 2017)
Alvar Aalto Light and Space (Petit Grand Publishing, 2013),
LIGHT SPACE in Finland (Petit Grand Publishing, 2009),
OYA STONE QUARRY amazing underground space (ZUISOSHA, 2010)

Photography &Text｜© Takashi Koizumi
Translation｜Haruki Makio[Fraze Craze Inc.]
　　　　　　Michiko Gunter, Kenneth Gunter
Chief Editor｜Shuichi Ishihara
Drafting｜Hiroshi Igata[kabutomushi]
Drafting Support｜Teruo Fujishita, Shogo Ushio, Seiya Inagaki,
　　　　　　　　Ayaka Nishimura
Pronunciation Supervision｜Lise Schou, Sakane Sirkku
Design｜Malpu Design Co.,Ltd.
Printer｜UENO PRINT Co.,Ltd.
Special Thanks｜Sr. Sheryl Chen (Tautra Mariakloster)
　　　　　　　 Weronica Olafsen Løland (Knarvik Church)

北欧モダンチャーチ＆チャペル 聖なる光と祈りの空間

2017年12月13日　第1刷発行　　First printing December 13, 2017

編集者｜石原秀一
発行者｜工藤秀之
発行所｜バナナブックス ©
　　　　株式会社トランスビュー

〒103-0007　東京都中央区日本橋人形町2-30-6
Tel. 03-3664-7333　　Fax. 03-3664-7335
http://www.transview.co.jp/

Chief Editor｜Shuichi Ishihara
Publisher｜Hideyuki Kudo
© Banana Books
TRANSVIEW Co.,Ltd.

2-30-6, Nihonbashi-Ningyocho Chuo-ku, Tokyo, 103-0007 Japan
Tel.+81-3-3664-7334　Fax.+81-3-3664-7335
http://www.transview.co.jp/

2017 BananaBooks, Printed in Japan
All rights reserved
ISBN978-4-902930-34-4